Affirmative Action

Kathiann M. Kowalski

This book is dedicated to my son, Christopher Meissner.

The author gratefully acknowledges the following people for their insights and assistance: Martin Kurtzweil, Harvard Law School, and The Andrew W. Mellon Foundation; Donnie Long, Cleveland Bar Association; Terrence Pell, Center for Individual Rights; and Laura K. Meissner. The author also benefited from the scholarship and teaching of her former professors, including Albert Sacks, Milton Katz, and Stephen Breyer at the Harvard Law School, and Howard Ball at Hofstra University. Last, but not least, she thanks her husband, Michael Meissner, and children, Chris, Laura, and Bethany Meissner, for their encouragement and support.

Marshall Cavendish Benchmark
99 White Plains Road
Tarrytown, NY 10591-9001
www.marshallcavendish.us

Copyright © 2007 by Marshall Cavendish Corporation
Maps Copyright © 2007 by Marshall Cavendish Corporation
Maps by XNR Productions, Inc.

All rights reserved. No part of this book may be reproduced or utilized in any form or by any means electronic or mechanical including photocopying, recording, or by any information storage and retrieval system, without permission from the copyright holders.

All Internet sites were available and accurate when sent to press.

Library of Congress Cataloging-in-Publication Data
Kowalski, Kathiann M., 1955-
Affirmative action / by Kathiann M. Kowalski.
p. cm. — (Open for debate)
Summary: "Outlines the arguments of those both for and against affirmative action programs and the history behind such programs"—Provided by publisher.
Includes bibliographical references and index.
ISBN-13: 978-0-7614-2300-3
ISBN-10: 0-7614-2300-1
1. Affirmative action programs—United States—History—Juvenile literature. 2. Discrimination in employment—United States—History—Juvenile literature. 3. Discrimination in education—United States—History—Juvenile literature. I. Title. II. Series.
HF5549.5.A34K69 2006
331.13'30973—dc22
2005028728

Photo research by Linda Sykes Picture Research, Inc., Hilton Head, SC.
Alex Wong/Getty Images: cover and pages 1, 2–3, 5, 6; Larry Downing/Corbis-Sygma: 15; Hulton Archive/Getty Images: 19; The Granger Collection: 22; Andrew Lichtenstein/Image Works/Time Life Pictures/Getty Images: 29; Khalil Bendib/*The Black Commentator*, Issue Number 49, July 3, 2003, www.blackcommentator.com: 38; AP/Wide World Photos: 44; National Archives/Time & Life Pictures/Getty Images: 66; Michael L. Abramson/Time & Life Pictures/Getty Images: 90; David Butow/Corbis Saba: 101; AP/Wide World Photos: 102; Paul Sancya/AP/Wide World Photos: 105; David Maxwell/AFP/Getty Images: 112.

Editorial Director: Michelle Bisson
Art Director: Anahid Hamparian
Series Designer: Sonia Chaghatzbanian

Printed in China
1 3 5 6 4 2

Contents

1 **Affirmative Action—Or Reverse Discrimination?** 7
2 **Historical Overview** 18
3 **Arguments for Affirmative Action** 37
4 **Arguments Against Affirmative Action** 59
5 **The Supreme Court and Affirmative Action** 78
6 **Moving Ahead** 97
  Notes 114
  Further Information 129
  Bibliography 132
  Index 136

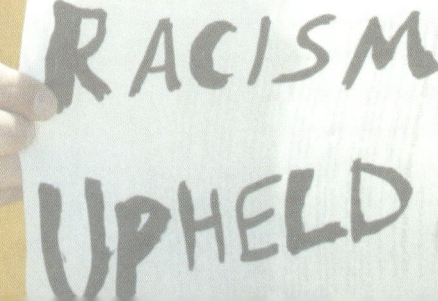

Defend
Affirmative Action
& Integration
Fight for Equality
MICHIGAN
RACISM
UPHELD

Affirmative Action— Or Reverse Discrimination?

When Boston University turned Michael Cox down for a job coaching its women's ice hockey team, he sued. The university's head hockey coach had previously informed Cox there was "a slight amount of pressure to strongly consider two females" for the job. The university claimed it was looking for the best and most talented coach for its women's team. But Cox's lawyer said the university was really discriminating against Cox because of his sex.

Affirmative action has provoked controversy for nearly fifty years now. Much of the debate centers on policy issues and arguments. But the debate is also deeply personal to many people. Some individuals feel profound thanks for the opportunities affirmative action has given them. Others feel deep resentment about so-called reverse discrimination.

Tough Cases

When a New Jersey school district decided to cut one teacher from its business department, the district faced a dilemma. Teachers Sharon Taxman and Debra Williams

Affirmative Action

had both joined the district's faculty on the same day. They had equal job qualifications, too. But Taxman was white and Williams was black. The school board decided to keep Williams so its business department would still have one minority teacher.

Taxman sued, saying that the school board unlawfully discriminated against her. The federal district court and the Third Circuit Court of Appeals sided with Taxman. The school board appealed, and the Supreme Court agreed to hear the case in 1997.

Shortly before oral argument, though, the school board agreed to settle the case. The settlement resolved the dispute between Taxman and the school district. But it left open the question of whether public employers can use race or various other factors as a "tie-breaker" in employment decisions.

For over twenty years, a federal court lawsuit sought to correct continuing patterns of segregation at Alabama's state universities. Among other things, the court decided that Alabama should increase black enrollment at its historically white colleges. It also ordered the state to increase white enrollment at its historically black colleges. In theory, that would boost those colleges' reputations statewide and draw more talent, funding, and other resources to improve the schools. And that would benefit all students attending those colleges—whether they were black, white, or of another ethnicity or race.

Toward that aim, District Court Judge J. Harold Murphy issued a 1995 order requiring the state to set up Diversity Scholarships at historically black colleges. The scholarships aimed to attract whites and other non-black students. However, graduate student Jessie Tompkins was not eligible to apply because he was African American. Because he needed more money for school, Tompkins had to take a year off from his studies.

The court eventually changed the scholarship so students

Affirmative Action—Or Reverse Discrimination?

of all races could apply. Meanwhile, however, Tompkins had to interrupt his education because a program meant to promote racial equality for African Americans as a group meant he could not get a particular scholarship as an individual.

In another case, a jury awarded $550,000 in damages to a white male police officer who said he had suffered racial discrimination. Specifically, the officer claimed that the mostly black city council in Inglewood, California, had unlawfully denied him a promotion because of his race. This case highlights the fact that ethnic groups that are in the minority in some parts of the country are in the majority elsewhere. What might be affirmative action in some areas, then, could in theory be discrimination against a minority somewhere else.

These are just a few cases that have come up in the debate over affirmative action. Often, parties on both sides have substantial arguments to support their positions. Court decisions do not always provide clear guidelines for deciding all cases, either. One thing is clear, though. Affirmative action is not just a theoretical issue. Rather, it has a real-world impact on many people.

What Is Affirmative Action?

Broadly speaking, affirmative action includes all positive steps taken to increase the representation of various groups in fields that historically have excluded them. Over the last five decades, affirmative action programs have aimed mainly to benefit racial and ethnic minorities, as well as women. However, affirmative action can benefit other groups, too, such as veterans of the armed services, the elderly, and the disabled.

Affirmative action programs operate mostly in three arenas. First, in the field of education, many colleges and universities aim to increase their enrollment of various

Affirmative Action

minority group members. Second, in the job market government employers and various companies hope to increase the hiring and promotion of various ethnic groups and women. And third, affirmative action can also come into play when doing business with the government.

Affirmative action includes publicity campaigns, recruitment visits, and other programs that encourage people in underrepresented groups to apply to schools, try out for a job, or bid on contracts. This type of affirmative action arouses the least controversy. In one sense, increasing the size of the applicant pool makes things more competitive. Yet people in the larger applicant pool still compete against everyone else.

Affirmative action also includes special programs to improve certain group members' ability to compete against others. For example, leadership training can help job applicants present themselves better. Mentoring programs pair newer trainees with more experienced role models. Skills workshops build expertise people need to perform well in a particular environment. Such programs raise some debate if they exclude either gender or certain ethnic groups outright.

The most controversy comes from programs that give people in targeted groups an actual preference over other candidates for a job, promotion, contract, or seat at a university. In other words, people in the targeted group get an actual edge over similarly qualified people just because they belong to that group. Sometimes programs spell out what that preference is. More often, programs refer to the preference as one factor among many that enter into final decisions.

Either way, such affirmative action preferences give members of certain groups real benefits based on race, ethnicity, gender, or other factors. And those benefits matter when it comes to dividing scarce resources. There just are

Affirmative Action—Or Reverse Discrimination?

not enough seats at prestigious universities, high-paying jobs, or profitable government contracts for everyone.

A Heated Debate

Affirmative action arouses intense emotions on both sides of the debate. Proponents of affirmative action see it as a way to remedy injustices in American society. Even though discrimination is now clearly against the law, many members of those groups continue to lag behind their white or male counterparts. The reasons for such lags are complex, and there are no quick and easy fixes.

In the meantime, affirmative action offers opportunities for talented individuals who otherwise might not fare as well in higher education, the job market, or in business. Supporters say it makes equal opportunity a reality for groups that still suffer substantial disadvantages and sometimes even outright discrimination. By leveling the playing field for everyone, supporters say, affirmative action promotes civil rights and social justice. At the same time increased diversity and greater opportunities can benefit society in general.

Opponents say affirmative action preferences are unfair. They agree that past discrimination was wrong, but they say two wrongs do not make a right. In their view, affirmative action is really reverse discrimination against people outside the groups the programs aim to help.

Critics of affirmative action note that America has an array of laws aimed at preventing and punishing unlawful discrimination on the grounds of race, sex, and nationality. They do not feel anyone should get special favors just because he or she happens to belong to a certain minority or gender. More fundamentally, critics oppose any classifications based on group membership rather than individual merit.

Beyond the pros and cons of affirmative action lies a

Affirmative Action

host of legal issues. No affirmative action program can stand if it violates principles in the Constitution. Because the Constitution is the supreme law in the United States, courts will strike down any programs that violate it.

The Fourteenth Amendment's guarantees of due process and equal protection of the laws are especially relevant:

> **No State shall make or enforce any law which shall abridge the privileges or immunities of citizens of the United States; nor shall any State deprive any person of life, liberty, or property, without due process of law; nor deny to any person within its jurisdiction the equal protection of the laws.**

Courts have interpreted this provision to forbid discrimination "under color of law" against people on the grounds of race, gender, religion, and national origin. Under color of law means that some government action is involved. Among other things, this would include actions such as government contracting, as well as hiring and firing within government agencies. It also includes conduct by public universities, which are owned and run by the government.

Beyond this, various laws forbid private persons from discriminating on the grounds of race, gender, religion, and national origin. For example, the Civil Rights Act of 1964 forbids discrimination in the workplace, as well as in public accommodations. The law applies to almost anyone engaged in interstate commerce, including most private businesses. It also applies to institutions that receive federal funding.

Other federal laws also protect employees from prejudice. The Equal Pay Act of 1963 says women and men who do substantially the same work in the same establishment deserve equal pay. The Civil Rights Act of 1991 allows employees to sue for damages for workplace

Affirmative Action—Or Reverse Discrimination?

discrimination. The Age Discrimination in Employment Act of 1967 forbids employment discrimination against people over age forty. The Americans with Disabilities Act of 1990 and the Rehabilitation Act of 1973 prohibit discrimination against people with various handicaps.

Antidiscrimination laws apply in the field of education, too. The Education Amendments of 1972 prohibit any school receiving federal funds from discriminating on the basis of gender. Those schools likewise cannot discriminate on the grounds of someone's race or ethnic group.

Affirmative action programs thus present a fundamental dilemma. When does a benefit to people in one group become unlawful discrimination against another?

Legal issues will be addressed in greater detail later. For now, though, it's important to note that the Supreme Court has allowed affirmative action programs in certain contexts. However, under the most recent court rulings, there must be a narrowly tailored, compelling interest for having such programs, especially where government entities are involved. Impacts on people outside the benefited groups must be limited. And courts will generally not allow quotas, or set numerical targets, under affirmative action programs.

Examining the Issue

In part, people's attitudes about affirmative action depend on what questions they're asked. Survey questions with terms like "preferential treatment" and "quotas" generally get less positive responses than questions involving "equal opportunity."

Views on affirmative action also differ, in general, by ethnic group. In one survey, whites were about twice as likely as blacks to agree strongly with the idea that blacks should overcome prejudice and work their way up without special favors—45 percent versus 23 percent. At the same

Affirmative Action

time, 21 percent of whites felt it was very likely a white person would be passed over for a job or promotion because of affirmative action.

Likewise, surveys show significant differences in how various ethnic groups think about racial equality in America. In a 2001 survey by the *Washington Post*, the Henry J. Kaiser Family Foundation, and Harvard University, between 40 percent and 60 percent of white people polled felt that blacks in America were faring at least as well as their white counterparts. Government statistics say otherwise, although many nonracial factors affect the figures, too.

In another study of racial issues in four large cities, 20 percent to 30 percent of whites surveyed felt there was little or no discrimination against blacks in America. Another 44 percent to 46 percent in each city said only "some" discrimination against blacks takes place. In contrast, between 57 percent and 69 percent of blacks in the same four-city study felt there was "a lot" of discrimination. Clearly, the two racial groups had dramatically different perceptions.

Of course, not all whites or blacks feel the same way on any issue. Some of affirmative action's most outspoken critics are persons of color. Among them are Supreme Court Justice Clarence Thomas, Ward Connerly of the American Civil Rights Institute, and talk show host Larry Elder. On the other hand, affirmative action has strong supporters among various whites, including William Bowen of the Andrew W. Mellon Foundation, Supreme Court Justice Ruth Bader Ginsburg, and Bob Laird, a former director of admissions for the University of California at Berkeley. Nonetheless, surveys of groups' perceptions provide useful insights.

Your own family background and experiences are likely to affect your views on affirmative action. You are a product of your family and ethnic background. Your neighborhood, school, and other factors will affect how

Affirmative Action—Or Reverse Discrimination?

SUPREME COURT ASSOCIATE JUSTICE CLARENCE THOMAS HAS BEEN AN OUTSPOKEN OPPONENT OF AFFIRMATIVE ACTION.

you approach the issue, too. Try to be aware of your own attitudes and predispositions as you explore the debate on affirmative action. At the same time, try to see the issue from other people's viewpoints.

Beyond this, try to see the debate over affirmative action in a broader context. For most of its history, the lion's share of benefits in the United States went to people of European descent. White Anglo-Saxon male Protestants usually had an "in" when it came to getting into the best schools, getting the best jobs, and leading the government. And they often took affirmative steps to keep others out.

Over the last several decades, though, America's demographic makeup has been shifting dramatically. As of 2003, white-only non-Hispanics made up about 68 percent of America's population. By 2050, white-only, non-Hispanic people will be only about half of the

A Black and White Case?

Less than two weeks after Eddie Jordan became New Orleans' first black district attorney, fifty-three white staff workers found themselves out of a job. About forty of those clerks, child-support workers, and investigators sued in federal district court. They claimed Jordan had discriminated on the grounds of race.

Jordan's lawyer, G. Phillip Shuler III, argued that the new district attorney had a right to hire and fire whomever he wanted. When Jordan took office, nearly 70 percent of New Orleans's population was black, while only 40 percent of the district attorney's office staff was black. Among the sixty-eight people hired during Jordan's first six months in office, however, 92 percent were black. During his campaign, Jordan had promised to increase the number of blacks working in the district attorney's office.

The white plaintiffs' lawyer, Clement Donelon, argued, "You can't go out, no matter how much you believe in affirmative action, and unilaterally create an affirmative action plan." The federal Equal Employment Opportunity Commission made a preliminary finding that race played a role in Jordan's actions. And evidence at the trial showed that many fired white staff workers had more experience and higher job interview scores than various black workers whom Jordan had kept or hired in their place.

During sixteen hours of deliberations, the jury of ten whites and two blacks sent the judge several questions. One asked if the law forbids firing large groups of whites "to achieve racial diversity."

On March 30, 2005, the jury delivered its verdict, finding that Jordan had unlawfully discriminated against forty-three white employees. The jury awarded the group approximately $1.9 million in back pay and other damages.

"I wasn't making racial decisions," Jordan insisted. His office announced it would appeal the verdict. Meanwhile, the plaintiffs' attorney was happy. "Race discrimination is wrong," Donelon said. "It goes both ways."

The plaintiffs in the Jordan case were not challenging a formal affirmative action plan. Instead, they alleged blatant racial discrimination by an individual. Nonetheless, the case presents many of the fears and frustrations surrounding the debate over affirmative action. How far can people or policy makers go to increase diversity in different settings? And what, if anything, can people who feel they have been discriminated against do about it?

Affirmative Action—Or Reverse Discrimination?

country's population. Meanwhile, Hispanics' percentage of the population will grow from about 13 percent in 2000 to 24 percent in 2050. Black-only Americans will increase by about two percentage points during those fifty years. And Asian-only Americans will increase from about 4 percent to 8 percent of the population.

Meanwhile, the United States will grow to a country of nearly 420 million people. America will face increased challenges of caring for its people's needs. That will require the talents and efforts of men and women from all sorts of ethnic groups.

Thus, today's debate about affirmative action is not just about who gets accepted into schools, hired for jobs, or offered contracts. It is about how to promote a fair chance for everyone to participate in all sectors of society. And, ultimately, it is about how America can maximize opportunities for all its people so the country can meet the challenges of tomorrow.

2
Historical Overview

Affirmative action programs as we know them are less than fifty years old. Yet discrimination has its roots much farther back in American history, and it continues to affect our society today. Developing informed opinions on affirmative action requires an appreciation of how it came about, and of how government support has varied over the years.

Enslaved and Subdued

Go back 230 years in American history when there was no such thing as affirmative action. Unless you were a white male landowner, your legal rights were rather limited.

During America's early years, most black people in the United States were slaves. The law treated them as property, and they had practically no rights. Owners forced slaves to work long, hard hours, in return for the barest minimum of food and shelter. Slaves generally could not go to school or even learn to read. They could not associate freely with each other. They did not even have the legal right to keep their immediate families together. And if

AFRICAN AMERICANS WERE NOT THE ONLY GROUP DISCRIMINATED AGAINST IN THE UNITED STATES. WOMEN HAD FEW RIGHTS IN THIS COUNTRY'S FIRST TWO CENTURIES. HERE, WOMEN AT A BOOTH ASK PASSERSBY TO VOTE YES ON WOMEN'S SUFFRAGE FOR A VOTE TO BE HELD IN OCTOBER 1915. WOMEN DID NOT WIN THE NATIONWIDE RIGHT TO VOTE FOR ANOTHER FIVE YEARS.

slaves tried to escape or otherwise displeased their owners, they suffered cruel and inhuman punishments.

In addition, various native tribes had already been pushed off their traditional homelands. And other tribes would soon suffer a similar fate.

Other ethnic minorities had few, if any, members within the country's existing boundaries until the middle of the nineteenth century. Those minorities who were in the United States at that time often encountered prejudice from the white Protestant majority ruling the country. Bigotry increased as waves of immigrants arrived in the United States, with groups like the Know-Nothing

Affirmative Action

Party discriminating against Catholics and foreigners.

Women also had few rights throughout the eighteenth and nineteenth centuries. Most states restricted women's rights to own and control property. Often, the law limited the type of work women could do outside the home, too.

In addition, many colleges and most professional schools would not admit women. And, of course, women did not win the right to vote across America until the Nineteenth Amendment was ratified in 1920. Even then, women continued to suffer harassment, unequal wages, and other discriminatory treatment.

In short, early America openly subdued blacks and minorities, as well as women. Instead, the law favored white males.

One Step Forward, and Then Back

The first major step forward came with the abolition of slavery. In 1863, President Abraham Lincoln issued the Emancipation Proclamation. That order freed all the slaves in the states fighting against the United States in the Civil War. Two years later, the Thirteenth Amendment abolished slavery throughout the United States. It provides that:

> **Neither slavery nor involuntary servitude, except as a punishment for crime whereof the party shall have been duly convicted, shall exist within the United States, or any place subject to their jurisdiction.**

The Fourteenth Amendment was ratified in 1868. It states that all persons born or naturalized within the United States are citizens of the country as well as the state where they live. It forbids states from enforcing any law that would "abridge the privileges or immunities of citizens of the United States." And it requires states to grant

Historical Overview

due process and equal protection of the laws to all persons within their jurisdiction.

The Fourteenth Amendment also changed the apportionment method for the House of Representatives and the Electoral College. Previously, only three-fifths of the slave population counted for those purposes. Now, all persons in each state count, except for those Native Americans who aren't taxed. The Fourteenth Amendment also disqualified people who had rebelled against the United States from holding public offices. That provision kept most of the South's former political leaders from holding office in the years immediately following the Civil War.

The Fifteenth Amendment followed in 1870. It provides that a citizen's right to vote "shall not be denied or abridged . . . on account of race, color, or previous condition of servitude."

All three amendments give Congress the power to enforce them through appropriate legislation. Thus, Congress passed laws aimed at guaranteeing the rights of freed slaves. For example, Congress overrode President Andrew Johnson's veto to pass the Civil Rights Act of 1866. That law made it a crime for anyone to interfere with someone else's civil rights, and it still remains in force today.

During this Reconstruction Era, Republican leaders from the North openly encouraged African Americans to run for public office. Indeed, many of the South's former white leaders were disqualified, and large numbers of black men were voting for the first time. Additionally, federal troops stayed in the South to prevent further rebellion. With their protection, many black candidates won elections to public office for the first time in American history.

At the same time, strong resentment was brewing in the South. Many whites did not accept the government's actions as measures to provide equal rights. Rather, they saw these actions as a way to punish the South for daring to rebel against the North. Southerners also resented "car-

Affirmative Action

DURING RECONSTRUCTION, MALE AFRICAN AMERICANS GOT THE RIGHT TO VOTE AND RUN FOR OFFICE. THE FIRST BLACK SENATORS (THEN CALLED "COLORED") ARE SHOWN IN THIS 1872 LITHOGRAPH BY CURRIER & IVES.

Historical Overview

petbaggers"—people who came down from the North to reap the spoils of war and to exploit the South's ruined economic position.

The presidential election of 1876 began a retreat from the advance of blacks' rights in the South. Although Democrat Samuel Tilden actually won more popular votes, ballot challenges in several states prolonged the electoral vote count. During that time, Republican and Democratic leaders secretly hammered out a deal that came to be known as the Compromise of 1877. Among other things, Republicans promised that Hayes would withdraw federal troops from the South if the results of the electoral investigation went their way. As a result, Hayes won the presidency by a single electoral vote.

With the end of the Reconstruction Era, Congress stopped championing the rights of black people. A further setback came when the Supreme Court overturned parts of Congress's last major Reconstruction Era law, the Civil Rights Act of 1875. Section 1 of that law had guaranteed equal access to inns, transportation, theaters, and other places of public amusement, without regard to any "previous condition of servitude." Under Section 2, anyone violating those rights could be fined $500 for each offense, or imprisoned for up to a year.

In 1883 the *Civil Rights Cases* interpreted the 1875 law as having been passed by Congress to enforce the Thirteenth Amendment. However, the Court did not view the denial of access to public accommodations as involving any "badge of slavery" or involuntary servitude. Moreover, the Court ruled that Congress had no right to regulate how private businesses treated former slaves. Beyond that holding, Justice Joseph Bradley wrote:

> **When a man has emerged from slavery . . . there must be some stage in the progress of his elevation when he takes the rank of a**

Affirmative Action

> **mere citizen, and ceases to be the special favorite of the laws, and when his rights as a citizen, or as a man, are to be protected in the ordinary modes by which other men's rights are protected.**

African Americans certainly got no favorable treatment in the Jim Crow period that followed the Reconstruction Era. Segregation became the rule throughout the South, as the federal government retreated from the civil rights arena. Literacy tests, poll taxes, and outright intimidation stripped most black Southerners of the right to vote and other rights guaranteed by the Constitution. Anyone who challenged the status quo risked retaliation, including painful death through lynching.

In 1896, the Supreme Court's decision in *Plessy v. Ferguson* upheld mandatory segregation of the races in public transportation. In effect, the Court blessed the status quo and the treatment of blacks as second-rate citizens.

Thus, instead of enforcing existing civil rights laws, the government openly encouraged inferior treatment of blacks and other people of color. Indeed, in many cases, the government actually required such discriminatory treatment. The U.S. military forces, for example, remained segregated through World War II. President Harry Truman eliminated military segregation in 1948.

The Civil Rights Era Dawns

By the middle of the twentieth century, activists were demanding equal rights for blacks and other minorities. Then in the 1954 case of *Brown* v. *Board of Education*, the Supreme Court held that "separate but equal" schools were inherently unequal. While school desegregation cases would continue for more than thirty years, *Brown* signaled a major change in the legal approach to civil

Historical Overview

rights. The case breathed new vitality into the Fourteenth Amendment.

Women were demanding equal rights, too. In 1960 women's work opportunities were mostly in low-paying factory and service jobs. Moreover, when companies did allow women to do the same jobs as men, about one-third of those companies had separate, higher pay scales for the men.

No wonder women's full-time earnings averaged just 60 percent of men's. Schools, companies, and even the mass media openly discouraged women from seeking better jobs. And various states still restricted women's abilities to sell property, enter into contracts, and conduct other business on their own. As minorities demanded equal rights, so did women.

Responding to public pressure, Congress passed new landmark civil rights laws. The Civil Rights Act of 1964 guaranteed blacks and other minorities equal access to public accommodations. In effect, the law restored the provisions that the Supreme Court had disallowed over eighty years earlier in the 1883 *Civil Rights Cases*. This time, though, the law had a firm foundation in both the Fourteenth Amendment and the interstate commerce clause of Article I of the Constitution. The law also drew support from the *Brown* case ruling that "separate but equal" is inherently unequal. The 1964 civil rights statute outlawed employment discrimination as well, plus discrimination by organizations receiving federal funds.

Congress and the states also took action to protect minorities' right to vote. The Twenty-fourth Amendment, ratified in 1964, made it unconstitutional to deny anyone the right to vote in federal elections on the grounds of failure to pay a poll tax or any other tax. The Voting Rights Act of 1965 added extra protections guaranteeing the right to vote.

Women made strides in their fight for equal rights, too.

Affirmative Action

Women had continued to suffer discrimination on the job and elsewhere, even after winning the vote. In 1963, however, the Equal Pay Act made it illegal for employers to pay different wages to men and women for substantially the same work at the same place of business. And Title VII of the Civil Rights Act of 1964 outlawed employment discrimination not only on the basis of race or ethnic minority, but also on the grounds of sex.

Title IX of the Education Amendments of 1972 was a huge step forward for women's rights in education. The law forbids schools receiving federal funds from discriminating on the basis of gender. If schools are found to be discriminating, they can lose their funding. Nonetheless, rules for enforcing Title IX did not go into effect until the late 1970s. Before then, many colleges limited admissions for women and gave the lion's share of scholarship money to men. Various law schools, medical schools, and other programs also had quotas restricting women to 10 percent or less of their enrollment.

In theory, the law now provided equal rights for both women and minorities. In practice, however, compliance was far from universal. Plus, there was still the question of how to address the lingering effects of past discrimination.

Affirmative Action Begins

Affirmative action at the federal government level began when President John F. Kennedy issued Executive Order 10925 in 1961. The order established the President's Committee on Equal Employment Opportunity and set forth an official policy of nondiscrimination in federal employment. Beyond that, the order called upon companies contracting with the federal government to "take affirmative action" to employ and treat applicants without regard to

Historical Overview

their race, creed, color, or national origin.

After Kennedy's assassination in late 1963, President Lyndon B. Johnson pushed hard for passage of the Civil Rights Act of 1964. Now federal law made it illegal for almost all private employers to discriminate against people based on race, ethnicity, or sex.

For Johnson, however, it was not enough just to stop discriminating against people of color. Rather, America needed something more to make the law's promise of equality a reality for the millions of people who suffered from a history of prejudice and racial hatred. That "something more" would be affirmative action.

On September 24, 1965, President Johnson issued Executive Order 11246. As before, it directed that, "The contractor will take affirmative action to ensure that applicants are employed, and that employees are treated during employment, without regard to their race, creed, color, or national origin." The order called upon contractors to document their efforts to ensure equal opportunity in hiring. The government could punish violations of the order by canceling contracts, barring companies from future contracts, and other measures. Additionally, Johnson's order gave the Secretary of Labor authority to investigate and take action on any complaints of discrimination. Two years later, Executive Order 11375 expanded Johnson's 1965 executive order to include women.

Specific goals for hiring women and minorities began under the administration of President Richard Nixon. When Nixon took office, workers in construction trades in the Philadelphia area were over 98 percent white. Accordingly, in 1969, Assistant Secretary of Labor Arthur Fletcher drafted Labor Department Order No. 4. Also called the Philadelphia Order, it required "special measures" to identify underrepresented groups and increase hiring among those groups. By 1971, the order's scope also

Affirmative Action

applied to contractors outside the construction industry and to women.

Affirmative action expanded more during President Jimmy Carter's administration. The Public Works Employment Act of 1977 required at least 10 percent of the money spent on certain types of federal projects to go to minority business enterprises (MBEs) and women business enterprises (WBEs).

The following year, Congress amended the Small Business Act to expand MBEs' federal contracting opportunities. As originally passed in 1958, section 8(a) of the law gave preferential treatment to small businesses that were "socially and economically disadvantaged." Under the 1978 amendments, companies owned by whites could still qualify if they could show facts supporting a claim of social and economic disadvantage. Now, however, companies with majority ownership by blacks, Hispanics, Asian Pacific Americans, or Native Americans automatically qualified for benefits offered to socially and economically disadvantaged businesses.

The section 8(a) contracting program extends to a broad range of government contracting programs. As a result, MBEs benefited from set-asides in a broad range of contracts dealing with defense, transportation, construction, and other areas. In other words, the presumption in favor of ethnic groups gave them a substantial leg up in the bidding process.

Over two hundred state and local governments also adopted programs to help MBEs and WBEs. Among other things, the laws provided training and funding, as well as set-asides in public contracting.

Meanwhile, affirmative action was growing in other arenas. Harvard became the first selective university with an affirmative action program to attract minorities in

Historical Overview

AFFIRMATIVE ACTION PROGRAMS SET QUOTAS FOR MANY BUSINESSES, AMONG THEM CONSTRUCTION COMPANIES. THIS AFRICAN-AMERICAN WORKER HOLDS A DRILL IN A BUILDING UNDER CONSTRUCTION IN A SET-ASIDE PROGRAM FOR MINORITY CONTRACTORS FUNDED BY A STATE GOVERNMENT IN THE 1990s.

Affirmative Action

1966. Soon, many universities were actively recruiting both women and minorities.

Affirmative action programs varied considerably. Schools with open admissions policies and relatively low admissions standards concentrated most of their efforts on getting minority students to apply. More selective universities faced a dilemma, however. They wanted more minority enrollment, but they also wanted to keep their admissions standards high.

Some programs used specific quotas, or set figures, that would come from underrepresented minority groups. Some schools had separate tracks for considering white and minority applicants. Still other schools gave a set number of extra points for applicants in minority groups. Yet other schools, like Harvard, did not say exactly how race or ethnicity would affect someone's chances of admission. Rather, they made it one of a mix of factors considered by the admissions committee in determining what students would add to the university.

Professional organizations encouraged similar efforts at the graduate school level. For example, the Association of American Medical Colleges (AAMC) aimed to get medical schools to have a 12 percent minority student enrollment by 1975. Although minority enrollment was only 10 percent by that date, the goal raised consciousness among schools and increased recruiting efforts. In 1990 the association set a new goal of admitting three thousand medical students from underrepresented groups by the year 2000. Although the results again fell short, the group's efforts have kept the issue at the forefront in schools' consciousness.

Some companies in the private sector also began affirmative action programs. Now that the law forbade discrimination in employment, some employers saw a new business opportunity for attracting talented minorities to their ranks. And some companies saw affirmative action as good public relations. Who wouldn't want to be known for giving minorities and women equal opportunities to advance along with their white or male counterparts?

Beyond this, many companies that did business with the federal and some state governments needed some form of affirmative action if they wanted to bid on contracts. Otherwise, they would not be able to comply with Executive Orders 11246 and 11375, or other contracting requirements.

The Pendulum Swings Back

During the 1980s, Presidents Ronald Reagan and George Bush resisted further expansion of affirmative action in government contracting. In addition, several court decisions overturned affirmative action programs. Even when courts upheld affirmative action, they closely examined the individual program's need, intent, and effects.

In 1978, the Supreme Court struck down an affirmative action admissions program at the University of California, Davis. Five justices objected to the medical school's quota system and dual-track admissions system. However, five justices also concluded that race could be used as a positive factor in the admissions process.

In 1979, however, the Court upheld a voluntary affirmative action plan hammered out by a steel company and its union. And in 1980, another case upheld the 1977 federal law that set aside at least 10 percent of the spending for certain construction projects for MBE contractors. Two more Supreme Court cases in 1987 upheld affirmative action plans, too.

In 1989, however, the Court held a 30 percent set-aside for MBEs unconstitutional in *City of Richmond v. Croson*. In response, various states and municipalities

"To Fulfill These Rights"

On June 4, 1965, President Lyndon B. Johnson gave the graduation speech at Howard University, a traditionally black university in Washington, D.C. These excerpts from Johnson's comments sum up his feelings on affirmative action:

> In far too many ways American Negroes have been another nation: deprived of freedom, crippled by hatred, the doors of opportunity closed to hope. . . .
>
> Freedom is the right to share, share fully and equally, in American society—to vote, to hold a job, to enter a public place, to go to school. It is the right to be treated in every part of our national life as a person equal in dignity and promise to all others.
>
> But freedom is not enough. You do not wipe away the scars of centuries by saying: Now you are free to go where you want, and do as you desire, and choose the leaders you please.
>
> You do not take a person who, for years, has been hobbled by chains and liberate him, bring him up to the starting line of a race and then say, "you are free to compete with all the others," and still justly believe that you have been completely fair.
>
> Thus it is not enough just to open the gates of opportunity. All our citizens must have the ability to walk through those gates.

This is the next and the more profound stage of the battle for civil rights. We seek not just freedom but opportunity. We seek not just legal equity but human ability, not just equality as a right and a theory but equality as a fact and equality as a result.

For the task is to give 20 million Negroes the same chance as every other American to learn and grow, to work and share in society, to develop their abilities—physical, mental and spiritual, and to pursue their individual happiness.

To this end equal opportunity is essential, but not enough, not enough. Men and women of all races are born with the same range of abilities. But ability is not just the product of birth. Ability is stretched or stunted by the family that you live with, and the neighborhood you live in—by the school you go to and the poverty or the richness of your surroundings. It is the product of a hundred unseen forces playing upon the little infant, the child, and finally the man . . .

The Negro, like [other minority groups], will have to rely mostly upon his own efforts. But he just can not do it alone.

Affirmative Action

developed fuller justifications for their set-aside programs or scaled them back substantially. Nonetheless, courts still aimed to limit state and local affirmative action programs. Among other things, federal courts struck down a Detroit program for promotions in the police department, as well as a Maryland program that dealt with state troopers.

In 1995, the Supreme Court announced that minority set-asides in federal contracting programs would also be subject to strict scrutiny. President Bill Clinton denied that the case, *Adarand Constructors, Inc. v. Peña*, was the death of affirmative action:

> **The Supreme Court has raised the hurdle, but it is not insurmountable. Make no mistake: the Court has approved affirmative action that is narrowly tailored to achieve a compelling interest. The constitutional test is now tougher than it was, but I am confident that the test can be met in many cases.**

Promising to "mend, not end" affirmative action, Clinton's administration re-examined various federal agencies' affirmative action programs. In 1997, the federal government revealed a more limited affirmative action policy targeted at particular industries where discrimination still existed. Following guidance from the Department of Justice, the government also revised its rules under section 8(a) of the Small Business Act. While the new rules still presumed that MBEs were at a disadvantage, other companies or parties could challenge that presumption through administrative procedures. Nonminority-owned companies also faced less significant burdens for showing that they might also qualify as socially or economically disadvantaged.

While all this was going on, the Fifth Circuit Court of Appeals overturned a two-track system for considering

Historical Overview

admissions applications at the University of Texas. That case, *Hopwood v. Texas*, forbade state universities in Texas, Louisiana, and Mississippi from considering race in the admissions process—at least until after the Supreme Court's rulings in two other cases in 2003. (Until the Supreme Court rules, federal court of appeals cases are directly binding only on the states within their circuits.)

A backlash against affirmative action was also brewing in the states of California and Washington. Led by African-American businessman Ward Connerly, the California Board of Regents ended the state's affirmative action programs. In 1996, California voters approved Proposition 209, which became Article I, Section 31 of the state constitution. Subsection (a) provides that:

> **The state shall not discriminate against, or grant preferential treatment to, any individual or group on the basis of race, sex, color, ethnicity, or national origin in the operation of public employment, public education, or public contracting.**

Washington voters approved an almost identical provision when they passed Initiative 200 in 1998.

At the urging of Governor Jeb Bush, Florida also outlawed consideration of race for admission to its state universities in 2000. Instead, it adopted the One Florida, also known as the Talented Twenty, Program. The top 20 percent of the class at each of the state's high schools would get guaranteed admission to one of the ten colleges within the state's public university system. This is one example of "percentage plans" intended to boost diversity in a race-neutral way.

Meanwhile, the Center for Individual Rights filed two lawsuits challenging affirmative action programs at the University of Michigan. In 2003, the Supreme Court

Affirmative Action

upheld the law school's program, but it overturned the program for the undergraduate arts and sciences college. The Court's decisions and rationales are examined later in this book, along with other key decisions. Before that, however, take a closer look at the policy arguments for and against affirmative action.

3
Arguments for Affirmative Action

At first glance, affirmative action seems to be an effort to make up for past injustices done to blacks, minorities, and women. Certainly those groups have all suffered discrimination in American society. And affirmative action does represent an effort to make things right.

However, affirmative action is not merely compensation for past wrongs. Likewise, it is naïve to think of affirmative action as something that springs from "white guilt." This is the concept that some well-to-do whites feel guilty about having so much when others are less fortunate, especially people of color. Though some people may feel that way, the characterization ignores the substance of arguments in favor of affirmative action.

Supporters of affirmative action say its aim is not payback for past wrongs. Rather, it is justice for America's present and future. What are the supporters' arguments?

Affirmative Action

A SATIRICAL COMMENT ON THE SUPREME COURT'S TAKE ON AFFIRMATIVE ACTION ON A WEB SITE CALLED BLACKCOMMENTATOR.COM.

Affirmative Action Promotes Diversity

Americans in the twenty-first century come from many cultural backgrounds. Projections show that the country will become even more diverse in the decades ahead. At the same time, Americans will have more frequent dealings with people from other countries and cultures around the world.

More and more, diversity is a fact of life in America. Champions of affirmative action programs see these programs as a way

Arguments for Affirmative Action

to foster diversity in different environments. And, at least in the education context, a majority of the Supreme Court has recognized diversity as a valid goal for affirmative action.

Institutions of higher learning must prepare young people to function well in our diverse society. Since today's students will be tomorrow's leaders, they should become sensitive to and be able to serve the needs of all types of Americans. Experts for the University of Michigan advanced this view in cases that came before the Supreme Court in 2003. In their view, diversity in higher education prepares students to be better citizens in America's democracy.

"Our whole democracy is improved by providing access to a diverse group of young people to institutions that are still very much pathways to political, social, and economic power," adds Martin Kurzweil, who researched and coauthored the book *Equity and Excellence in American Higher Education* while serving as a researcher at the Andrew W. Mellon Foundation. Affirmative action opens doors that let people exercise real power in society. Giving people a genuine say in America's future is consistent with the country's democratic ideals.

Elite colleges and universities offer substantial benefits to all their students. If they didn't, then the competition to get in wouldn't be so intense. "Students who attend selective schools (including racial minorities who would not be there without admissions preferences) have access to incredible resources and networks that provide returns for the rest of their lives," notes Kurzweil. "Beyond this," he adds, "every student who attends a racially diverse institution benefits from the exposure to peers from different backgrounds and with different perspectives."

Thus, while students who get preferential treatment benefit from what the university offers, all other students benefit from learning in an environment with people from many different backgrounds. Such exposure to a

Affirmative Action

range of perspectives gives students new experiences and broadens their intellectual horizons. It also shakes students out of any preconceptions or intellectual comfort zones. All this helps develop critical thinking skills. As a result, educators say, students become more actively engaged in the educational process.

To provide a rich educational experience, most colleges and universities want a culturally diverse student body. Students likewise appreciate the opportunity to interact with people from diverse backgrounds and experiences.

"The beginning for me was when I realized that not everyone shares the same views as I, and that our different cultures have a lot to do with that," one white student told researchers at the University of Michigan. Similarly, three-fourths of the students in an Oregon State University study supported the concept of diversity in education.

However, various minorities are still underrepresented, especially at selective institutions. To make up for that, schools use affirmative action. It becomes a tool to enhance the social and intellectual atmosphere so that all students may benefit.

Businesses and professions are also aware of the benefits of diversity. Different perspectives in a diverse workplace add to innovation and creativity. Businesses profit from the varied viewpoints and analyses that people from different genders and cultural backgrounds bring to the table.

Diversity also helps businesses meet the demands of the global marketplace. Diversity in management and in the workforce helps businesses understand and meet customers' needs. This, in turn, helps them make profits and stay competitive.

Moreover, customers in today's marketplace expect companies to measure up to various social standards. In other words, they value social responsibility and want to see companies promote equal opportunity. Companies that earn high marks for diversity get good press reports. *Black*

Arguments for Affirmative Action

Enterprise magazine, for example, publishes lists of firms that score high marks for having a strong representation of minorities throughout the company ranks. Doing business with minority-owned suppliers is also considered a plus.

Indeed, if a company is not diverse, clients may take their business elsewhere. "From a dollars-and-cents standpoint, it is no longer economically realistic for companies to be lily-white and male," Theodore Shaw of the NAACP told the *New York Times*.

Leaders in a variety of professions likewise favor affirmative action. Among other things, greater diversity can help underserved groups. Thus, having more doctors or lawyers from minority groups may increase those groups' access to health care or legal services.

Toward this end, the Association of American Medical Colleges has been urging schools to enroll minority students since at least 1970. Having more competent physicians from minority groups should help meet the needs of patients in those groups who presently receive poor care.

However, greater diversity in professions is not just about helping underserved groups. As in academic institutions, minority and women professionals bring a broader perspective to the field. They add to the richness of practicing in a particular area. And, by increasing the pool of potential candidates, greater diversity adds to the overall quality of excellence in any field.

On a broader scale, advocates say, the economy as a whole benefits from affirmative action. To be competitive in today's world, America simply cannot ignore the talents of large segments of its population. Former President Bill Clinton summed up this sentiment in 1995, when he vowed to "mend, not end" affirmative action:

> **When affirmative action is done right, it is flexible, it is fair, and it works. . . .**

Affirmative Action

> **When we allow people to pit us against one another or spend energy denying opportunity based on our differences, everyone is held back. But when we give all Americans a chance to develop and use their talents, to be full partners in our common enterprise, then everybody is pushed forward.**

In short, when affirmative action opens doors for people, everyone benefits.

Affirmative Action Counters Ongoing Discrimination

Discrimination is not a thing of the past, say champions of affirmative action. Some Americans still harbor hatred for certain groups. Sometimes that bigotry is open and apparent.

For example, employees at a maintenance shop for the North Carolina transportation department displayed a noose. The white workers meant to mock the civil rights movement and to show approval of past lynchings of black people during the Jim Crow era. Despite black workers' complaints, the shop's white supervisors let the noose stay up for over a month.

A New York firefighter also found a noose hanging on his equipment. Similar incidents took place in Florida, Missouri, and Washington. All these offenses took place in the twenty-first century—not in the distant past.

Women also still experience discrimination. Sometimes employers promote men over women. Other times, women suffer sexual harassment. Many seek relief by filing complaints with the Equal Employment Opportunity Commission, but others do not. They try to work things out themselves. Or they just don't want to "rock the boat."

Sometimes, discrimination is much more subtle. Employers might deny putting a woman on a "mommy track"

Arguments for Affirmative Action

without her approval. But they may promote male employees faster for their outstanding devotion, good client relations, or other intangible factors. Other women bump up against a "glass ceiling." They get hired and promoted to a certain point. Yet despite their best efforts, they cannot advance to the top levels of management.

Again, proving discrimination would be hard. If asked to explain, employers would justify their actions with subjective criteria, such as superior client relations or outstanding interpersonal skills. Such factors are clearly important to businesses, but they are hard to measure objectively. Success in those areas depends largely on the views of the evaluator, who is often male. Supervisors also influence success in client relations by working younger associates into relationships with longstanding clients over time. Consciously or not, male supervisors may give younger female associates fewer opportunities to work with major clients.

Not all workplaces are like this. Indeed, many companies have excellent records. Nonetheless, many women are still fighting an uphill battle against chauvinism and stereotypes.

Remarks by Harvard University president Lawrence Summers in early 2005 show what many women are up against. In discussing why women are underrepresented in high-level science fields, Summers argued that women are just not as interested in making the sacrifices required to do the work. Anyway, he claimed, men have more "intrinsic aptitude" for complex science. (He resigned effective summer 2006, in resonse to continuing controversy.)

Summers didn't outright deny any woman a job or promotion with those remarks. And, after a national media uproar, he named Evelynn Hammonds as Harvard's new senior vice provost for diversity. He also pledged support for a $50 million program to improve conditions for women at the university over the next decade. Yet women still felt the sting of Summers' initial criticism, as well as perceived hostility from others in the academic world.

Affirmative Action

FORMER HARVARD PRESIDENT LAWRENCE SUMMERS CAUSED AN ANGRY UPROAR WHEN HE MADE REMARKS INDICATING THAT WOMEN'S INEQUALITY TO MEN IN SCIENTIFIC AND MATHEMATICAL ABILITY WOULD EXPLAIN WHY THEY WERE NOT PROMOTED IN EQUAL NUMBERS TO MEN.

Arguments for Affirmative Action

Affirmative action does not automatically stop discrimination and harassment. For that, society still needs vigorous enforcement of its civil rights laws, plus a more enlightened public. Nonetheless, supporters say, affirmative action can counter some of the hostility so women and minorities feel more welcome in business and academia.

Affirmative Action Battles Bigoted Attitudes

Even if people won't admit it, prejudice probably plays a big part in people's opposition to affirmative action. Bob Laird argues that many people publicly lie about their true feelings about race.

Indeed, people may not even be aware of their prejudices. In a psychology test devised by Anthony Greenwald at the University of Washington, people often found it easier to link women's names with home-related words than with career-related words. Test subjects may have unconsciously bought into the "traditional" notion that a woman's place is in the home.

In other studies, test subjects are often quicker at linking black faces with negative words than with positive words. Researchers say this shows an implicit, or hidden, bias against black people. Numerous studies in America have also found implicit bias against Latinos, Asians, Jews, and other groups. Likewise, surveys show that ethnic names often trigger stereotypical attitudes.

These test results do not necessarily result in racist or chauvinistic actions. What they show, however, is that people can hold negative attitudes about groups even when they don't realize it. That could unconsciously influence decisions about who gets a job, a contract, or enrollment at a competitive school.

Additionally, many people prefer to hire candidates who resemble them. Sometimes the resemblance relates to

Affirmative Action

drive, common experiences, or other factors. But white males in leadership positions may unconsciously rely on physical appearances, too.

"It is well documented that conscious and unconscious race bias, even rank discrimination based on race, remain alive in our land, impeding realization of our highest values and ideals," wrote Supreme Court Justice Ruth Bader Ginsburg. Affirmative action prods people to move beyond whatever attitudes and assumptions they may hold about others. Supporters say this can offset bias that people otherwise face.

Affirmative Action Helps Level the Playing Field

Even if discrimination were all in the past, both women and minorities still lag behind white men in various fields. Affirmative action aims to correct some of the harm done by past discrimination. As civil rights advocate Martin Luther King Jr. argued:

> **It is impossible to create a formula for the future which does not take into account that our society has been doing something special *against* the Negro for hundreds of years. How then can he be absorbed into the mainstream of American life if we do not do something special *for* him now, in order to balance the equation and equip him to compete on a just and equal basis?**
>
> **. . . For it is obvious that if a man is entered at the starting line in a race three hundred years after another man, the first would have to perform some impossible feat in order to catch up with his fellow runner.**

Without doing something more, affirmative action supporters say, patterns set during past discrimination will

Arguments for Affirmative Action

continue. "Basing present discrimination on past discrimination is obviously not right," said former President Jimmy Carter.

Although several decades have passed, it is naïve to think that we live in a color-blind society, says William Bowen, the president of the Andrew W. Mellon Foundation. Instead, policy makers should acknowledge the long-lasting effects of America's "unlovely history" and eliminate them.

Prolonged racial and ethnic discrimination tore at the fabric of family structure. It limited people of color to segregated neighborhoods with poor schools and shabby housing. It closed people out of schools and professions. It limited talented individuals' chances for advancement. These and other factors dragged people down, and our society can still see the consequences.

"The position of the Negro today in America is the tragic but inevitable consequence of centuries of unequal treatment," wrote Supreme Court Justice Thurgood Marshall in a case dealing with racial preferences for medical school. He added:

> **In light of the sorry history of discrimination and its devastating impact on the lives of Negroes, bringing the Negro into the mainstream of American life should be a state interest of the highest order. To fail to do so is to ensure that America will forever remain a divided society.**

Statistics show a startling divide between whites, on the one hand, and people of color, on the other. In 2003, 10.5 percent of all white Americans were living in poverty, for a total of about 24.3 million people. About 9.1 million blacks and almost the same number of Hispanics lived in poverty that same year.

Although the total numbers were smaller, the percentages of poor blacks and Hispanics were 24.3 percent and

Affirmative Action

22.5 percent, respectively. Thus, black and Hispanic Americans are twice as likely as whites to live in poverty. Inferior educational opportunities, fewer job prospects, and higher crime rates are just a few problems that plague poverty-stricken neighborhoods.

Meanwhile, the "average" white family earns more than average families in other ethnic groups. In 2003, the median family income for white Americans was about $46,000, versus about $30,000 for blacks and $33,000 for Hispanics. "Median" means that half the data in the group are above that number, and half are below.

Net worth statistics show even more disparities. Net worth reflects not just income, but also savings, investments, home ownership, and other factors. In 2000, the median net worth for non-Hispanic white American households was $79,400. For black households, median net worth was just $7,500, and for Hispanics, it was $9,750. Both groups fared far worse than whites.

In most respects, women have caught up to their male counterparts at the undergraduate college level. Yet women are still underrepresented in various graduate and professional fields. And they still face obstacles in the workplace. As of 2003, American women's incomes averaged barely 76 percent of men's median incomes. This is a significant improvement over the period from 1960 to 1980, when women typically earned just 60 percent of what men earned. Yet it is still a far cry from equality. Even when women and men have the same qualifications and job experience, women still make about one-third less than men overall.

Why do differences in income and net worth matter? Wealthier people can generally afford to live in better school districts that have more resources for their children. Alternatively, they are better able to afford private-school tuition and whatever educational benefits those schools offer. Higher-income families also have more time and resources for activities that enrich their children's back-

Arguments for Affirmative Action

grounds and experiences.

Greater economic resources lead to better scores on college admission tests. In 2004, students from families earning over $100,000 a year had an average combined SAT (Scholastic Aptitude Test) score of 1115, out of a total possible score of 1600. Students from homes with reported family incomes between $40,000 and $50,000 had an average score of 989. Teens whose families earned between $10,000 and $20,000 had an average score of just 887. The overall average was 1026. Such differences in scores may be one reason selective colleges and universities typically draw just 11 percent of their incoming classes from the lowest quarter of family incomes, even when those schools have need-blind admissions policies and "full-need" financial aid policies. ("Need-blind" admissions policies consider students' applications without regard to whether they can pay tuition. "Full-need" financial aid policies supply the full difference between school expenses and the amount the financial aid committee believes that a student's family should pay.)

Economics is not the only factor at work. Among students who gave information about their ethnicity, the average combined math and verbal score in 2004 was 1059 for whites, 857 for blacks, and between 909 and 926 for Hispanic groups. Different experiences and expectations throughout grade school and high school probably play a huge role in these groups' overall performances.

Members of minority groups may also experience a "stereotype threat" during standardized tests, suggests Bob Laird. When the stakes are high, test takers in some ethnic groups know people expect them not to do as well as other groups. Nervousness about that can affect test scores—thus making the expectation a reality.

Disparities also exist when it comes to getting high-paying jobs or landing government contracts. Top management at American companies continues to be overwhelmingly white and male. Likewise, as of 2001, whites owned about

Affirmative Action

85 percent of American businesses, with black and Hispanic ownership at around 4 percent and 6 percent, respectively. Minorities are also underrepresented in high-paying professions, such as engineering, medicine, and law.

Women also continue to face obstacles in the workplace and professions. Engineers, for example, are still predominantly male. And though women are now well represented in law school classes, top-earning partners at the nation's prestigious law firms are still mostly men. Women also hold only a small percentage of the nation's top corporate positions.

For both women and minority groups, advocates say affirmative action opens up opportunities. This, in turn, helps counter disadvantages people in those groups otherwise face.

Affirmative Action Counters White Male Privilege

Antiracist activist Tim Wise says that the flip side of discrimination is privilege. He argues that white males in America have enjoyed racial and gender preferences for hundreds of years.

For example, the first Naturalization Act in 1790 granted citizenship benefits only to free white persons. The Homestead Act of 1862 mostly helped white people buy land cheaply. And, of course, whites were not slaves or subject to the Jim Crow laws passed in the late nineteenth century.

Such privileges continued into the twentieth century. Federal housing and loan policies frequently favored people in white neighborhoods. At the same time, black borrowers often got turned down for home loans in "declining" black neighborhoods. And they were often "redlined," or excluded, from moving into white neighbor-

Arguments for Affirmative Action

hoods. As a result, 96 percent of the 28 million people who moved to U.S. suburbs between 1950 and 1966 were white.

More recently, notes Wise, about 80 percent of the growth in new jobs has been in America's suburbs. While redlining and other blatant discrimination has ended, suburbia in the United States is still mostly white. Thus, whites have the advantage of being closer to those new jobs.

In contrast, a 2005 study by Robert Wagmiller at the University of Buffalo found that physical isolation makes it especially hard for many poor black men in America to get work. They don't have cars to drive to work, and public transportation often doesn't take them from their city neighborhoods to suburban jobs. This prevents them from improving their economic and social situation.

Whites are also more than twice as likely as blacks to inherit money or other property from relatives. Plus, when white people do inherit money or property, they tend to receive far more than minorities. Combined with disparities in income, this brings a typical white family's net worth to almost eleven times more than that of an average black family, and eight times more than an average Hispanic family. This wealth translates into yet more privileges for white Americans, argues Wise.

Similarly, women have often missed out on privileges that similarly situated men have enjoyed. Though Supreme Court Justice Sandra Day O'Connor graduated third in her Stanford Law School class, for example, she had trouble finding a law firm willing to hire her because she was a woman. Even today, women are underrepresented in various professions and top corporate positions.

Women and minorities often also lack the benefits that informal "good old boy" networks have long given their white male colleagues. These unstructured systems have advanced men's careers with mentoring, social contacts, and business networking. Even though women and minorities

Affirmative Action

may now have desks in the office, they may still be excluded from these informal networks. This can hamper their ability to excel in business development, client relations, and other areas that are critical to advancement.

In short, white males as a group have long enjoyed competitive advantages they did not earn. Without affirmative action, the system would continue to favor them.

Just as a wheel alignment keeps a car from pulling to one side or the other, affirmative action aims to steer our social and economic system straight again. As Justice David Souter argued in his dissent in *Adarand Constructors, Inc. v. Peña*:

> The Court has long accepted the view that constitutional authority to remedy past discrimination is not limited to the power to forbid its continuation, but extends to eliminating those effects that would otherwise persist and skew the operation of public systems even in the absence of current intent to practice any discrimination.

Affirmative action supporters say American society is skewed in favor of white males. Affirmative action should be able to correct that by taking race, ethnicity, and gender into account in reasonable ways.

Affirmative Action Promotes Fairness in the Distribution of Public Benefits

Public employees and public contractors are not just doing a service for the government. They receive substantial benefits, too. H. George Frederickson at the University of Kansas's Policy Research Institute has argued that affirmative action can and should alter how government distributes those benefits so as to help disadvantaged groups.

Generally speaking, the public wants government to perform both economically and efficiently. Based on avail-

Arguments for Affirmative Action

able resources, the government is expected to provide the public with the best quality service for the least amount of dollars. However, argues Frederickson, the government should also promote social equity. In other words, it should properly adjust public benefits to respond to the needs of citizens and their different situations.

Under this view, the government can and should give greater benefits to disadvantaged groups. Accordingly, set-asides, bonuses, or other preferences in public contracting would give those groups a realistic opportunity to compete in the marketplace, thus countering social and economic inequities.

One can make the same argument about government employment. In that context, affirmative action can help people in disadvantaged groups get good government jobs with benefits. The experience gained through such employment can also help individuals become more competitive if they later look for jobs in the private sector.

Affirmative Action Serves the Public Good

In a more general sense, former Berkeley admissions director Bob Laird argues that affirmative action promotes "the greatest good for the greatest number." By moving toward the goal of a fully integrated society, America becomes a stronger democracy and a more just society.

It is true that for anyone who benefits from a racial preference, someone else is passed over. At the university level, William Bowen calls this the "opportunity cost" of accepting any particular student. Likewise, hiring or promoting an employee or awarding a contract usually means that someone else did not get the job. However, affirmative action supporters say, tough competition already means that no one has a vested interest in getting a particular university seat, job, or contract.

Don't Sidestep the Issue

Minority preferences are not the only way to improve the situation. But, supporters say, it is more efficient than other methods of dealing with the vestiges of discrimination.

For example, affirmative action advocates like William Bowen, Martin A. Kurzweil, and former Hamilton College president Eugene Tobin feel students from lower socioeconomic backgrounds should benefit from a "thumb on the scale" in the college admissions process. Yet they feel institutions should still use minority preferences, too. Kurzweil explains:

> **For simple reasons of demographics, socioeconomic status and race are not perfect substitutes. While minorities are disproportionately represented among the poorest applicants to selective colleges, the vast majority of poor applicants are non-minorities. So, if you were to simply give preference on the basis of socioeconomic status, the share of students from minority backgrounds would drop—by about half, according to our estimates.**

As another alternative to minority preferences, some colleges use "percentage plans" to increase diversity. But such plans increase minority representation only if elementary and high schools are largely segregated. Plus, they often don't result in admission to the most elite schools, so those universities' student bodies are less diverse.

Affirmative action supporters say it makes little sense to use surrogates, or substitutes, for race and ethnicity. Instead, we should meet the issue head-on and take ethnicity into account along with other factors. Bowen argues that this is the most "sensible and efficient" approach. Kurzweil adds:

> **For a variety of social and economic reasons, racial minorities do not achieve the standard credentials that would make them competitive applicants for admission at selective schools. While it is crucial to improve the conditions that underlie this credential deficit, in the meantime, it is crucial that selective colleges continue to diversify their student bodies through admission preferences.**

Affirmative Action

At elite colleges and universities, for example, Bowen and former Harvard president Derek Bok have argued that minority preferences have a negligible effect on non-minority applicants. In their book *The Shape of the River*, Bowen and Bok found that getting rid of all minority preferences at highly selective schools would slash black enrollment between 50 percent and 70 percent. In contrast, white applicants' admissions chances would rise just 1 percent or 2 percent in the 1200–1299 SAT ranges. Given the many factors that can influence admissions decisions, affirmative action supporters feel this effect is insignificant.

Elizabeth Anderson at the University of Michigan agrees that integration should be a compelling justification for affirmative action. When affirmative action brings people into schools and jobs, it embraces them in the mainstream of society. Barriers that separate people break down, and doors of opportunity open.

At the same time, integration through affirmative action forces coworkers, business associates, or fellow students to deal with women and minorities in new ways. As society becomes more integrated, people learn to treat others as individuals. And over time, that breaks down stereotypes and bigotry.

Affirmative Action Beneficiaries Are Just as Deserving

Harvard Law School professor Lani Guinier and Columbia Law School professor Susan Sturm disagree strongly with the idea that test scores make any student or job applicant more deserving than another. They feel that test scores do not adequately predict how people will ultimately do at a job or in school. In addition, tests may have built-in biases. Thus, test scores should not be the only or

Arguments for Affirmative Action

even the main yardstick for measuring out education and job opportunities.

Indeed, by definition, highly selective colleges and universities have the luxury of picking and choosing among their applicants. Even someone with a 4.0 grade point average and combined verbal and math SAT scores of 1500 or more cannot count on getting into any particular elite school. No one is guaranteed admission. At the same time, elite schools have the freedom to construct their classes based on a range of criteria beyond grades and standardized test scores.

Similarly, in the workplace, many factors enter into deciding which candidate will be the best person for any job. Some of those criteria are objective, such as test scores or length of experience. Yet subjective factors enter in, too, including drive, personality, and fit with the workplace's culture. Again, no one has an absolute right to a particular job or promotion.

Viewed in this light, affirmative action helps schools, employers, and contracting agencies look beyond simplistic criteria. They deserve the freedom to pick people who will best serve their missions and goals from a pool of qualified applicants.

Beneficiaries of affirmative action have important talents, skills, experiences, and perspectives. As they can benefit from being at an elite university or landing a plum job, others get the advantage of having them on board. Champions of affirmative action thus feel that program beneficiaries are just as deserving as others.

Affirmative Action Is Temporary

Affirmative action supporters agree that an ideal world would be color-blind. Yet the prejudices of the past continue to have effects today. Affirmative action supporters say it provides a much-needed temporary boost to its beneficiaries.

Affirmative Action

However, society must first take positive steps to help groups—especially minorities—that have suffered discrimination. As Supreme Court Justice Ruth Bader Ginsburg has argued, "The stain of generations of racial oppression is still visible in our society, and the determination to hasten its removal remains vital."

Groups that benefit from affirmative action would almost certainly prefer the same advantages that other groups in American society already enjoy. When that day truly comes, proponents will be more than glad to see the sunset of affirmative action. That day is not here yet, however.

4
Arguments Against Affirmative Action

Opponents of affirmative action sometimes come under attack for their motives. One charge is that they don't want to see minorities or women get ahead. Unfortunately, bigotry and chauvinism are not dead in our society, and some individuals probably do feel that way.

Still others claim that those who oppose affirmative action must be afraid of giving anyone else a competitive edge. Self-interest and insecurity may well explain some people's objections. However, policy debates are rarely advanced by ad hominem attacks—charges that malign individuals and their motives, instead of addressing the merits of their positions.

In fact, most serious critics of affirmative action insist that they support equal opportunity. They feel that affirmative action shortchanges that goal and hurts both its intended beneficiaries and other groups. Instead, they would prefer to see decisions about school admissions, employment, and contract awards made solely on a color-blind, gender-blind basis. After all, the Constitution guarantees everyone equal protection under the law.

Affirmative Action Is Discrimination

America's civil rights laws were a long time in coming. As the law now stands, however, all men and women are supposed to be equal before the law. The Fourteenth Amendment and federal statutes clearly forbid discrimination based on race, nationality, or gender. Critics say affirmative action runs counter to that mandate.

The law should be "color-blind," say people who oppose affirmative action. As Supreme Court Justice John Harlan wrote in *Plessy* v. *Ferguson* in 1896, "Our Constitution is color-blind, and neither knows nor tolerates classes among citizens." Harlan was in the minority at the time, and *Plessy*'s "separate but equal" holding was later overturned. Critics of affirmative action thus say the law should fully adopt Justice Harlan's position and be color-blind across the board.

Indeed, critics argue, distinctions made by affirmative action may increase tensions between groups. People see themselves as either inside or outside the groups that benefit. Issues of ethnicity or gender become matters of "them versus us," especially when the law blesses the distinctions. To quote Justice Harlan again, "[T]he common government of all shall not permit the seeds of race hate to be planted under the sanction of law."

Put another way, affirmative action programs favor some groups at the expense of others. That is bound to breed resentment and nurture hatred. At the very least, affirmative action keeps people conscious of factors like race, ethnicity, and gender. That can keep longstanding resentments alive.

Arguments Against Affirmative Action

Affirmative action foes say it doesn't matter that programs intend to help members of particular groups. In their view, the law has no "good cause" exception for discrimination. Indeed, Supreme Court Justice Anthony Kennedy wrote, "Policies of racial separation and preference are almost always justified as benign, even when it is clear to any sensible observer that they are not."

Regardless of the intent, affirmative action still treats people differently because of the color of their skin, their nationality, or their gender. That is wrong, argued Supreme Court Justice Antonin Scalia:

> **To pursue the concept of racial entitlement—even for the most admirable and benign of purposes—is to reinforce and preserve for future mischief the way of thinking that produced race slavery, race privilege and race hatred. In the eyes of government, we are just one race here. It is American.**

Despite any good intentions, affirmative action's distinctions presume that people in certain groups cannot make it on their own. This fuels prejudiced people's feelings that those groups are inferior. As Justice Sandra Day O'Connor wrote in a 1989 case striking down subcontractor set-asides in Richmond, Virginia:

> **Classifications based on race carry a danger of stigmatic harm. Unless they are strictly reserved for remedial settings, they may in fact promote notions of racial inferiority and lead to a politics of racial hostility.**

(A stigma is a label of shame or inferiority.)

Affirmative action can also insult groups that are held to a higher standard. As Supreme Court Justice John Paul Stevens noted in the same case, "[I]t stigmatizes the disadvantaged class with the unproven charge of past racial discrimination. . . ." In other words, a higher standard may

Affirmative Action

make people feel as if they are branded as being bigots or chauvinists, even if they never did anything wrong.

Hostility builds when people outside the favored groups see themselves as missing out. By definition, if a program gives any advantage based on race, ethnicity, or gender, then people outside those favored groups are missing out on something. Thus, the flip side of affirmative action for one group is discrimination against another.

Two wrongs do not make a right, say critics of affirmative action. They do not like America's history of racism and sexism, and they deeply regret the hurt it has caused. Instead of continuing to make racial or gender distinctions, however, critics of affirmative action want to move forward with equal treatment for everyone.

Past discrimination against one group should not justify present discrimination against any other groups, say affirmative action opponents. The act of making distinctions based on race or gender lies at the heart of past discrimination. To continue making distinctions now, even with good intentions, fails to uphold the ideals of equal protection. As Justice Antonin Scalia argued in a 1989 case overturning a city's affirmative action plan:

> **Racial preferences appear to "even the score" (in some small degree) only if one embraces the proposition that our society is inappropriately viewed as divided into races, making it right that an injustice rendered in the past to a black man should be compensated for by discriminating against a white. Nothing is worth that embrace.**

Affirmative Action Does Not Treat People as Individuals

The Constitution does not guarantee civil rights for groups. Rather, it promises basic freedoms and liberties to individual citizens. Thus, say critics, people should be

Arguments Against Affirmative Action

treated as individuals, not lumped together in any particular group. As Justice William Douglas wrote in a case in which a law school denied admission to a white male, "Whatever his race, he had a constitutional right to have his application considered on its individual merits in a racially neutral manner."

Affirmative action supporters often argue that any actual detriment to people outside the target groups is very small. For example, getting rid of affirmative action programs might increase white high school seniors' chances of getting into an elite college by less than two percentage points.

However, critics of affirmative action resist measuring impacts on a group as a whole. Rather, they look at the effect on an individual. If a black student with a B-minus average can get into an elite school while a white student with higher grades and an otherwise comparable background gets a rejection letter, affirmative action critics see that as unfair discrimination.

Moreover, critics say affirmative action degrades a person's individual value. Programs rely on assumptions that people in different groups generally hold certain viewpoints. Or they assume people in some groups have faced certain obstacles, while others have enjoyed various privileges. Either way, affirmative action relies on stereotypes.

Statistics may well show that people in certain ethnic groups are more likely to come from poor backgrounds or less likely to score high on some standardized tests. However, statistics describe groups of people, not individuals. They should not give some people greater legal rights than others.

Think about it this way. You can calculate the average height for all students in a classroom. But individuals still vary greatly from short to tall. Likewise, individuals' backgrounds, viewpoints, and abilities vary widely within any

Affirmative Action

ethnic or gender grouping. The law should thus treat people as the individuals they are.

Affirmative Action Runs Counter to the Merit System

Critics of affirmative action say it skews the whole merit system. Generally, people feel school admissions, jobs, promotions, contracts, and other benefits should go to the people who most deserve them.

For better or worse, students applying to colleges take standardized tests. The tests do not predict how well students will fare in their chosen fields after college. Nor do they necessarily forecast how well they will perform in college itself. All else being equal, however, most college admissions officers would prefer the candidate with a higher test score.

To be sure, standardized tests are not the only factor college admissions officers rely upon. They consider the courses taken in high school, community involvement, essays, and recommendations. They rely heavily on grades, too.

Nonetheless, college admissions officers know that high schools vary greatly in the quality of their teaching, students, and grading systems. An "A" does not mean the same thing at every school or in every course. Thus, most competitive colleges want an objective way to compare candidates. Standardized tests are not perfect, but they are the best colleges have so far.

Similarly, government agencies and companies often use exams to determine eligibility for hiring, promotions, and so forth. Again, the tests are not a perfect way to gauge future success. But the premise is that, all else being equal, the person who scores higher on the relevant exam is the one who should be chosen.

Likewise, government contract awards generally result from a public bidding process. Unless exceptions apply,

Arguments Against Affirmative Action

the lowest bidder wins and does the work. In theory, the bidding process helps the government function efficiently. It gets the job done right at the least cost to taxpayers.

The very use of tests, bidding procedures, or other requirements implies that the tests measure merit. But when those tools get pushed aside to let someone get ahead because of minority group status or gender, critics say that is unfair to the people who get passed over.

It shakes people's confidence in the overall process, as well. If tests, grades, or other factors are insignificant enough that they can be ignored for racial or gender preferences, why bother relying on them in the first place?

If institutions apply standards for some people, they should apply them for everyone. Otherwise, quality can suffer, and the whole system seems arbitrary and unfair.

Affirmative Action Should Not Demand "Compensation" from Innocent Parties

Yes, the American legal system allowed slavery and blessed discrimination against blacks, minorities, and women. But no living Americans own slaves now, and most of them played no direct role in evils like lynching or mandatory segregation. Thus, critics see little sense in making later generations of whites pay for the evils done in the past century.

Indeed, millions of white Americans did not even have family members in the United States until the great waves of immigration that came after slavery ended. When immigrants arrived from Europe in the late-nineteenth and early-twentieth centuries, they often found themselves closed out of jobs, crowded into slums, and otherwise victimized by discrimination. Despite that, most of them succeeded in building new lives here.

Immigrants from Asian countries ran up against prejudice, too. Many suffered discrimination in the workplace,

Affirmative Action

In World War II, Japanese-American citizens were forcibly removed from their homes and interned in camps as though they were prisoners of war although they had not committed any crimes against the U.S. government. Decades later, the government compensated those citizens and their survivors. Affirmative action critics sometimes point to Japanese and other Asian Americans as examples of "model minorities" who have achieved significant success as a group without preferential treatment.

Arguments Against Affirmative Action

housing market, and elsewhere. The U.S. government even imprisoned thousands of people during World War II for no reason other than the fact that they were Japanese American.

While Asian Americans are still a minority of the population, some affirmative action programs do not benefit them. Indeed, various colleges and universities treat Asian Americans as an "overrepresented" group. Yet, as with other groups, not all Asian Americans are the same. Indeed, many still encounter obstacles similar to those facing Hispanics or African Americans.

In contrast, some protected minority group members are themselves recent arrivals in America. They may face significant challenges in building a new life in this country. However, their situation did not result from America's history of racial and ethnic discrimination. Any "corrective" rationale for affirmative action simply does not apply to them.

Affirmative Action Hurts Its Supposed Beneficiaries

Affirmative action may propel some individuals into desirable jobs, elite universities, or lucrative contracts. However, critics say, affirmative action ultimately hurts even the people it aims to help.

One criticism is that affirmative action stigmatizes people. The idea is that other people will assume that minority group members or women got their positions only because of affirmative action. Consequently, they will look down on them.

Affirmative action will then blind others to the genuine contributions of minorities and women. It also waters down the achievements of individuals who would have succeeded solely on their own merits.

It is true that affirmative action does not do the work

Affirmative Action

for students, employees, or contractors. Yet even when people perform well, critics worry that affirmative action will make them doubt their own worth. Instead of feeling good about what they have done, the so-called beneficiaries of affirmative action may doubt whether they really deserve to be where they are. They may buy into the idea that, were it not for affirmative action, they would not be where they are today.

That is just not so, argues conservative commentator Larry Elder. A successful lawyer who attended a prestigious law school through an affirmative action program would not otherwise have been a bricklayer. He or she would most likely have gone to a different, less selective law school. Yes, the starting salary might have been slightly lower. But with sufficient drive, hard work, and talent, that person would probably still turn out to be a professional and financial success. Conversely, without hard work, talent, and drive, affirmative action will not make anyone into a superstar.

If anything, getting rid of affirmative action may actually improve some people's chances for success. Writing in the *Stanford Law Review*, Richard Sander reported that half of black law students were in the bottom 10 percent of their classes after the first year, versus just 5 percent for whites. Those students were also twice as likely to quit law school. Affirmative action thus seemed to create a "mismatch" between schools' demands and students' abilities.

Wide disparities happen at undergraduate colleges, too, the Education Trust reported in 2005. While schools varied widely, graduation rates for minority students lagged behind at many schools. At Ohio State University, for example, only 44 percent of minorities actually graduated within six years.

"Any racial group that's admitted under a separate, lower academic standard is going to lag in its academic performance once the students show up," adds Terrence

Arguments Against Affirmative Action

Pell, president of the Center for Individual Rights (CIR). "It's a function of the double standards in admissions. It does not reflect racial abilities."

Basically, all the students must compete with each other once school starts. To the extent that grades and test scores predict anything about college performance, students who came in under lower standards will have trouble competing with students who met higher standards. This is especially true when professors grade on a curve, where final grades reflect each student's performance relative to the class as a whole.

Thus, while various colleges have increased their minority enrollment, critics say this comes at the cost of minority students' success. Critics would rather see students go to less elite schools where they could succeed on their own. With better grades and a more solid educational foundation, they would improve their chances of getting into graduate school, landing good jobs, and so on.

Indeed, the end of affirmative action in public universities did not keep minority students from going to college in California after 1997. But, argues Elder, it did send students to schools where their academic credentials better matched schools' overall standards. If anything, overall minority enrollment in the state's public university system went up slightly.

Affirmative action not only downplays individuals' real achievements, but it implies that its target groups otherwise have little hope for succeeding in American society. Instead of helping group members move forward, it reminds them that no one expects them to do well anyway.

Ward Connerly believes that affirmative action can hinder minority group members, rather than help them. Affirmative action repeatedly stresses that America is "racist," that various minorities cannot do well on tests,

Affirmative Action

and that those groups cannot succeed without outside help. When young black children hear this, Connerly argues, it "prevent[s] those children from ever making the connection between that open door of opportunity and individual liberty and freedom."

In other words, affirmative action fosters minority group members' continued view of themselves as victims. It reinforces the belief that they cannot get ahead on their own. It allows people to blame society for their problems. It absolves them of individual responsibility for their actions and achievement. And it lets them off the hook for doing anything to improve the situation through hard work and wise choices.

Supreme Court Justice Clarence Thomas summed up the objections to "racial paternalism" in *Adarand Constructors, Inc. v. Peña*:

> **So-called "benign" discrimination teaches many that because of chronic and apparently immutable [unchangeable] handicaps, minorities cannot compete with them without their patronizing indulgence. Inevitably, such programs engender attitudes of superiority or, alternatively, provoke resentment among those who believe that they have been wronged by the government's use of race. These programs stamp minorities with a badge of inferiority and may cause them to develop dependencies or to adopt an attitude that they are "entitled" to preferences. . . .**
>
> **In my mind, government-sponsored racial discrimination based on benign prejudice is just as noxious as discrimination inspired by malicious prejudice. In each instance, it is racial discrimination, plain and simple.**

> **Arguments Against Affirmative Action**

Affirmative Action Does Not Solve Underlying Problems

Minority groups indeed face significant disadvantages in America. But, critics say, affirmative action will not cure those problems. If anything, it makes matters worse.

Racial double standards hide the fact that some ethnic groups are not achieving and succeeding in American society as well as others. "In fact, it delays and impedes our ability to address the problem head on," argues Terrence Pell. "Addressing it head on requires a variety of efforts by a lot of different players. And the only way to focus everybody's attention on that problem is to take away the Band-Aid that's used to cover it up."

Look at affirmative action for minority groups at colleges and universities. Schools have such programs in order to increase enrollment among members of groups that are "underrepresented." But those programs do not deal with why fewer members of those groups would otherwise get admitted.

One drawback might be that various minority students did not have the supportive family environment or enjoy the same economic security as other children. If so, then critics of affirmative action feel it would be more productive to focus on those factors.

Many elementary, middle, and high schools also fail to provide adequate preparation for college. A 2004 study by the Urban Institute found that various groups of minority high school students fell far behind white and Asian students in their rates for graduating from high school. The high school graduation rate was near 75 percent for whites and Asian Americans. Nationwide, however, only about half of Hispanic, Native American, and black children were graduating from high school. Instead of spending limited

Affirmative Action

resources on affirmative action programs at the university level, it might make more sense to improve the educational environment for all students at the lower grade levels.

Indeed, affirmative action programs help only a small percentage of people in minority groups. Even then, the programs' effects are imprecise. Many talented minority group members could attend quality schools or get good jobs even without affirmative action.

Other people who benefit may not deserve any extra edge. For example, a young black man may get a seat at an elite university. But if that student comes from an upper middle-class home with two parents, does he really deserve an edge over a white woman with comparable grades who grew up in a single-parent household with fewer resources?

Affirmative action programs also have limited impact. They help the individuals who get seats at elite schools, better jobs, or lucrative contracts. Beyond that, any benefits to the preferred group come from a "trickle down" effect. In other words, someone who gets a better job because of affirmative action can afford to live in a better neighborhood, build up wealth, and send his or her children to better schools. That, in turn, should help some members of the next generation to compete better in society. Meanwhile, the rest of the group gets little or nothing. Critics of affirmative action feel this is an inefficient way to deal with social problems.

Indeed, affirmative action programs may be more a way for institutions to help themselves than to help others. When elite universities set very high admissions standards, argues Pell, they know many minority group applicants won't meet those standards. Affirmative action helps universities avoid or deflect political attacks accusing them of being biased or racist. The institutions thus maintain an image of being both highly selective and socially responsible. Meanwhile, minorities admitted under lower standards of-

> **Arguments Against Affirmative Action**

ten struggle in classes where they must compete with students who met the regular high admissions standards.

Why Help Only Needy People from Certain Groups?

Why should affirmative action programs single out people in certain minority groups for favorable treatment? Although minority group members are more likely to face certain economic hardships in America, people in other groups face those problems as well.

As of 2003, about nine million blacks were living in poverty, as well as about nine million Hispanic people. But about 25 million people living in poverty were also white. And while over half of blacks and Hispanics earned less than $35,000 each year, so did more than one-third of whites.

Though whites do better on average than various ethnic groups, it is unfair to assume that any particular white person is better off than any individual minority group member. In fact, the lack of money may be one reason minority college students' college graduation rates are so low, aside from any arguments about "mismatches" from affirmative action. At Canisius College in New York, for example, whites and minorities graduate at similar rates once socioeconomic factors are taken into account.

Critics of affirmative action would prefer to see help go to everyone who faces economic or other disadvantages, regardless of the color of their skin. Thus, college admissions programs could aim to attract greater numbers of low-income students. Greater financial aid and more realistic assessments of parents' expected contributions would help more lower-class and middle-class students finish college without mounting up huge debts.

Indeed, Supreme Court opinions on affirmative action

Affirmative Action

say policy makers should generally use "race-neutral" ways to address issues before turning to racial and ethnic classifications. Critics of affirmative action feel race-neutral and gender-neutral programs are the only fair approach.

Engineering Any Racial Balance Is Wrong

Affirmative action may well be a sincere effort to make society better. Nonetheless, say critics, ideas about how America ought to be should not interfere with any individual's right to equal treatment.

Critics especially bristle when affirmative action programs rely too heavily on alleged underrepresentation in various fields. The fact that 60 percent of an area's residents belong to one ethnic group does not mean that 60 percent of the workers or students in different fields should come from that group. The law requires equal opportunity, not proportional representation in all walks of life.

In one unsuccessful challenge, the Center for Individual Rights argued that the Department of Housing and Urban Development was taking just such an approach. For one job category, the agency's hiring and promotion goals for Asian males relied on a difference of just one-tenth of a percentage point between the workforce representation and the civilian labor force—3.4 percent versus 3.5 percent. At that point, affirmative action programs seemed to be splitting hairs, rather than promoting justice.

Taken to extremes, affirmative action could lead to absurd results. Should Chicanos get first crack at government jobs if they as a group are poorer than other ethnic groups? Should states waive some requirements so more of their lawyers could be people of color? Supreme Court

Arguments Against Affirmative Action

Justice William Douglas posed these questions and warned:

> **The State, however, may not proceed by racial classification to force strict population equivalencies for every group in every occupation, overriding individual preferences. The Equal Protection Clause commands the elimination of racial barriers, not their creation in order to satisfy our theory as to how society ought to be organized.**

In short, the law guarantees all individuals fair and equal treatment under the law. Policy makers should not stray from that requirement based on their notions of how the world ought to work.

Affirmative Action Is No Longer Needed

Even if affirmative action was once appropriate, critics say it was never intended as a permanent solution. Rather, affirmative action was meant as a temporary measure to help victims of discrimination catch up.

Women have made significant strides in the last fifty years. While some professional schools or science programs still aim to attract more women, most colleges and universities have done away with any preferences they once gave women in admissions. Women's strong credentials and their overall performance in schools have shown that they don't need special treatment to succeed.

Similarly, while women are still underrepresented in some industries, female professionals are now common in many business and professional fields. Employers are well aware of the need to provide equal opportunity and avoid harassment. Yet with qualified women in so many fields, employers often do not need to give female job candidates any special edge. And while some women complain about

Choosing What to Challenge

Litigating an affirmative action challenge all the way through appeals can cost up to $3 million. Few people can afford that kind of money. Many lawyers won't take on cases alleging discrimination or challenging affirmative action programs on a contingency basis, where they would get a share of whatever someone might ultimately recover. The lawyers may not want to take on the risk of failure. Public interest law firms offer another way to get into court.

"What we can do is put these cases in a broader perspective," explains Terrence Pell, President of the Center for Individual Rights (CIR). Among other things, this conservative group has challenged a variety of affirmative action policies.

Instead of dwelling mostly on individual facts, Pell says, public interest law firms can focus on policy questions, such as whether racial preferences make sense and whom they help or hurt. Representation by a public interest law firm can also make the opposing party take the claim more seriously.

How does CIR choose which cases it will take to challenge affirmative action policies? "We want a case that makes this issue real for people," says Pell. "So in order to do that we have to find a case that is real, where an individual who would have gotten in didn't get in as a result of a policy that's used broadly by many universities. That's what makes a good public debate."

For the 2003 Supreme Court cases dealing with affirmative action at the University of Michigan, for example, CIR chose plaintiffs Jennifer Gratz, Patrick Hamacher, and Barbara Grutter from approximately two hundred rejected applicants who had contacted state lawmakers. With solid academic credentials and extracurricular activities, all three presumably would have gotten in if they weren't white.

In contrast, CIR usually turns down cases that don't present new issues of law. It also will not take cases that hinge on one person's wrongful actions, versus a broader institutional policy.

"The basic problem with that kind of case is even if you win it, the holding you get doesn't apply to anybody else," explains Pell. "We're looking for cases that challenge things that a lot of universities do as a matter of policy."

Arguments Against Affirmative Action

a glass ceiling or other obstacles, many women now hold important positions in the business world.

Today's high school seniors applying to college did not attend schools that were unlawfully segregated by race. Yes, school systems vary greatly in quality and resources. However, that holds true for many districts that have mostly white students, as well as those that are primarily black or Latino.

Likewise, civil rights laws have been in place for decades to protect people against discrimination in the job market. The Equal Employment Opportunity Commission reviews complaints, and the government can take legal action against companies that discriminate. In addition, private attorneys litigate claims charging racial, ethnic, and gender discrimination. Class action lawsuits can be especially costly, so companies have strong incentives to obey the law. Critics say minorities or women do not need the added boost of affirmative action programs to help them get and keep a job.

When champions of affirmative action point to cases of discrimination against minorities or women, critics say such cases show the system is working. In other words, when discrimination takes place, people have legal routes for seeking relief. Affirmative action critics do not see a need to give any extra relief based on racial, ethnic, or gender categories.

5
The Supreme Court and Affirmative Action

The Supreme Court has looked at affirmative action at schools, in the workplace, and in public contracting. Just as public opinion is widely split on the issue, so are the Supreme Court's decisions.

The *Bakke* Case and University Admissions

In 1978, the Supreme Court issued its first decision on the merits of affirmative action at a public university. The University of California, Davis, medical school had twice rejected white applicant Allan Bakke. However, the medical school had set aside sixteen of its one hundred entering class seats for minority and disadvantaged students. Some of those admitted students had significantly lower scores than Bakke.

By a vote of five to four, the Supreme Court struck down the medical school's admissions quotas in *Regents of the University of California v. Bakke.* Justices John Paul Stevens, Warren Burger, William Rehnquist, and Potter

The Supreme Court and Affirmative Action

Stewart found reasons to strike down the program under federal civil rights statutes. They did not make any findings on Bakke's constitutional challenges.

William Brennan, Byron White, Harry Blackmun, and Thurgood Marshall would have upheld the school's admissions program. They felt it was a proper way to remedy disadvantages from past prejudice. In their view, it did not go against the Constitution.

Justice Lewis Powell provided the swing vote to strike down the two-track admissions program. He felt a university could properly make certain racial or ethnic distinctions to promote its academic interests in diversity. Nonetheless, he felt the school's automatic set-aside of sixteen seats for minorities went beyond what the Constitution allowed.

"Racial and ethnic distinctions of any sort are inherently suspect and thus call for the most exacting judicial examination," began Powell. Even "benign" discrimination to help minorities was not exempt from the Fourteenth Amendment. Indeed, helping certain groups meant restricted opportunities for people outside those groups. Powell noted, "[T]here is a measure of inequity in forcing innocent persons . . . to bear the burdens of redressing grievances not of their making."

To justify using the "suspect classification" of race in admissions, Powell felt the government should have to show a substantial and constitutionally permissible purpose. Additionally, racial classifications would have to be necessary to accomplish or safeguard that goal. In Powell's view, that's where the medical school's quota system failed.

States have a "legitimate and substantial interest" in dealing with "the disabling effects of identified discrimination," noted Powell. However, there was no finding of prior identified discrimination.

Nor did the school need to reserve minority student

Affirmative Action

seats to promote better health care for minority patients. "Preferring members of any one group for no reason other than race or ethnic origin is discrimination for its own sake," wrote Powell.

That being said, Powell did not rule out all affirmative action programs. Specifically, a university's academic freedom was tied to the First Amendment's freedoms of speech and association. That freedom extended to the medical school's interest in "the attainment of a diverse student body" in order to promote "a robust exchange of ideas." Powell felt that the interest in diversity "clearly is a constitutionally permissible goal for an institution of higher education."

However, reserving a set number of seats was not the only way to attain diversity. In Harvard's more flexible program, for example, race could be one of several factors that tip the balance in an applicant's favor. Thus, the Court struck down the Davis medical school's racial quotas. But it left the door open for other, more flexible programs.

Correcting Manifest Imbalances

In 1979, the Court upheld a voluntary affirmative action plan hammered out by Kaiser Aluminum and the United Steelworkers of America. Among other things, *Steelworkers v. Weber* considered why white workers overwhelmingly outnumbered blacks in skilled craft jobs. Under the national agreement, at least one-half the trainees for new positions in those crafts would be black until the percentage of black skilled craftworkers at a plant was close to that of the local labor force.

"[T]he Kaiser-USWA plan is an affirmative action plan voluntarily adopted by private parties to eliminate traditional patterns of racial segregation," noted Justice William Brennan in the Supreme Court's majority opinion.

The Supreme Court and Affirmative Action

Although Justices Burger and Rehnquist argued that the plan was an unconstitutional quota system, the majority felt that the company and union did not violate the Constitution or federal civil rights laws by working to remedy past discrimination.

Beyond this, the Steelworkers' plan did not "unnecessarily trammel the interests of the white employees." The company did not fire white workers to replace them with blacks. Nor were whites barred from all advancement. Plus, the plan was a "temporary measure." It did not aim to maintain any specific racial balance, "but simply to eliminate a manifest racial imbalance."

The issue of correcting manifest imbalances came up again the following year. *Fullilove* v. *Klutznick* upheld the 10 percent set-asides for MBEs under the Public Works Employment Act of 1977. Among other things, less than one percent of all federal procurement money had gone to MBEs in 1976, even though minorities made up 15 percent to 18 percent of the population.

In his opinion announcing the Court's decision, Chief Justice Warren Burger wrote that assuring access by the minority business community to public funds is a constitutionally valid purpose. In his view, Congress did not have to act in a "wholly 'color-blind' fashion." The MBE provision's "strictly remedial measure" passed constitutional muster.

Nor did the existence of some burden on nonminority firms render the MBE program invalid. The provision might well disappoint some nonminority firms in their expectations. However, Burger wrote, "The actual 'burden' shouldered by nonminority firms is relatively light in this connection when we consider the scope of this public works program as compared with overall construction contracting opportunities."

Even if the nonminority firms were "innocent of any discriminatory conduct," Burger wrote, Congress could properly assume those businesses "may have reaped

Affirmative Action

competitive benefit over the years from the virtual exclusion of minority firms from these contracting opportunities."

Justice Lewis Powell's concurring opinion echoed this sentiment. In his view, any "marginal unfairness to innocent nonminority contractors" was "not sufficiently significant" to outweigh the government's interest in remedying the effects of past discrimination. Justices Marshall, Brennan, and Blackmun felt the set-aside provision also helped prevent "invidious discrimination" by the government. In other words, the government would not help keep discrimination alive by going along with the status quo.

Nonetheless, the Court remained divided. Justice John Paul Stevens argued that the law setting aside $400 million in contract funds for MBEs was a "random distribution of benefits on racial lines." Despite the intent to move beyond traditional prejudices, he feared that the law could lead to "automatic acceptance of new classifications" based on assumptions about groups as a whole.

Affirmative action proponents won additional victories in 1987. *United States* v. *Paradise* upheld an affirmative action plan imposed by a lower federal court. For nearly forty years, the Alabama Department of Public Safety had kept blacks from being hired as state troopers. To remedy that violation of the Fourteenth Amendment, the lower court's orders imposed hiring quotas. Also, the state would have to promote one black state trooper for every white state trooper it promoted. By a vote of six to three, the Court upheld the lower court's remedial orders.

Also in 1987, *Johnson* v. *Transportation Agency* upheld an affirmative action plan under which Santa Clara County promoted a qualified woman to a dispatcher job, even though a male's test scores were slightly higher. Before that, women held none of over 238 positions in the relevant job classification.

By a vote of six to three, the Supreme Court held the agency appropriately considered the successful job candi-

The Supreme Court and Affirmative Action

date's sex as one factor in her favor. The agency plan dealt with traditionally segregated job categories. Plus, the plan did not set rigid quotas. Rather, the agency adjusted its goals each year.

Moreover, no one had an absolute entitlement to any promotion based on sex, ethnicity, or anything else. Indeed, five other candidates besides Johnson lost out on the job. They all kept their current jobs and remained eligible for other promotions.

Stricter Scrutiny

In 1989, however, the Court swung back the other way. *City of Richmond* v. *Croson* held that a city's 30 percent set-aside for MBE contractors was unconstitutional. The city argued that its set-aside plan properly addressed widespread discrimination that had previously taken place in the construction industry. As an indirect result of that systemwide discrimination, less than one percent of its prime construction contracts had gone to minority businesses from 1978 to 1983. In contrast, Richmond's population was 50 percent black.

Despite those arguments, Justice Sandra Day O'Connor wrote, no direct evidence showed that the city or its prime contractors had discriminated against MBEs. Moreover, any guess as to how much business would have gone to MBEs with no discrimination by society at large was "sheer speculation." There was no logical link between the 30 percent quota and any specific injury from discrimination.

Just saying that a program had a benign or compensatory purpose was not enough to satisfy the Constitution. "Absent searching judicial inquiry into the justification for such race-based measures, there is simply no way of determining what classifications are 'benign' or 'remedial' and what classifications are in fact motivated by illegitimate

Affirmative Action

notions of racial inferiority or simple racial politics," Justice O'Connor wrote.

The city could have used race-neutral devices to increase contracting opportunities for small entrepreneurs of all races, she added. It could have made the bidding process easier. It could have relaxed financial responsibility requirements. It could also have offered training or financial aid to disadvantaged firms.

Justice Antonin Scalia took a more restrictive view. He felt states could make racial classifications only to undo their own past discriminatory conduct. Scalia also quoted from a book by Yale professor Alexander Bickel, *The Morality of Consent*:

> **[A] racial quota derogates [detracts from] the human dignity and individuality of all to whom it is applied. . . . Its evil lies not in its name, but in its effects: a quota is a divider of society, a creator of castes, and it is all the worse for its racial base, especially in a society desperately striving for an equality that will make race irrelevant.**

"Since blacks have been disproportionately disadvantaged by racial discrimination, any race-neutral remedy aimed at the disadvantaged *as such* will have a disproportionately beneficial impact on blacks," Justice Scalia added. "Only such a program, and not one that operates on the basis of race, is in accord with the letter and the spirit of our Constitution."

Justice Marshall dissented, joined by Justices Brennan and Blackmun. Business as usual without affirmative action could continue discriminatory patterns from the past, Justice Marshall feared.

> **More fundamentally, today's decision marks a deliberate and giant step backward in this Court's affirmative-action jurisprudence. . . . The majority's unnecessary pronouncements will inevitably discourage or prevent govern-**

The Supreme Court and Affirmative Action

mental entities, particularly States and localities, from acting to rectify the scourge of past discrimination.

In Justice Marshall's view, the city's "localized, industry-specific findings" were more than enough to justify a program to remedy "the *continuing exclusion* of minorities from a historically tight-knit industry."

Justice Blackmun also wrote a separate dissent. He found it ironic that the Court would not let Richmond, "the cradle of the Old Confederacy, . . . lessen the stark impact of persistent discrimination."

Meanwhile, other 1989 decisions made it harder to sue employers for alleged discrimination. One case made it harder for plaintiffs to prove employer discrimination. Another case limited when people could bring discrimination claims. Another case made it harder to settle discrimination cases involving large numbers of people. Yet another case limited local governments' liability for discriminatory acts by their employees. For the most part, the Civil Rights Act of 1991 countered the effects of these other decisions.

Affirmative Action Allowed in Broadcasting

In 1990, *Metro Broadcasting, Inc. v. FCC* came before the Supreme Court. By a vote of five to four, the Court upheld a Federal Communications Commission (FCC) policy that gave preferences to minority broadcasters. The FCC had adopted the policies consistent with laws that Congress passed during the 1980s.

Justice William Brennan's majority opinion viewed the policies as a "benign racial classification." Congress had found that "[T]he effects of past inequities stemming from racial and ethnic discrimination have resulted in a severe underrepresentation of minorities in the media of mass communications." Moreover, the FCC argued that the policies promoted programming diversity.

Affirmative Action

A majority of the Court agreed that "[E]nhancing broadcast diversity is, at the very least, an important governmental objective and is therefore a sufficient basis for the Commission's minority ownership policies." Not every minority broadcaster would hold different views or add to diversity in programming. However, the Court deferred to the agency's view that, on the whole, more minority ownership would lead to more diversity in broadcasting.

Moreover, the majority felt, any burden on nonminorities was "slight." Applicants had "no settled expectation" that they would get a broadcasting license "without consideration of public interest factors such as minority ownership."

Writing for the dissenters, Justice Sandra Day O'Connor argued that the Court should have used strict scrutiny to review the agency policies. In her view, an "important" interest in broadcast diversity was not enough to justify discrimination. Justice O'Connor also stressed that the Fourteenth Amendment's guarantee of equal protection under the law is an individual right.

> **At the heart of the Constitution's guarantee of equal protection lies the simple command that the Government must treat citizens "as** *individuals*, **not 'as simply components of a racial, religious, sexual or national class.'" Social scientists may debate how peoples' thoughts and behavior reflect their background, but the Constitution provides that the Government may not allocate benefits and burdens among individuals based on the assumption that race or ethnicity determines how they act or think.**

The FCC was wrong to assume that people thought in a particular manner based upon their race, O'Connor felt. Beyond that, the concept of any "benign" racial classification was "a contradiction in terms."

> **Governmental distinctions among citizens based on race or ethnicity, even in the rare**

The Supreme Court and Affirmative Action

> **circumstances permitted by our cases, exact costs and carry with them substantial dangers. To the person denied an opportunity or right based on race, the classification is hardly benign. The right to equal protection of the laws is a personal right, securing to *each* individual an immunity from treatment predicated [based] simply on membership in a particular racial or ethnic group.**

Justice Anthony Kennedy's dissent likewise criticized the Court for failing to follow a strict scrutiny standard of review. He added:

> **The perceptions of the excluded class must also be weighed, with attention to the cardinal rule that our Constitution protects each citizen as an individual, not as a member of a group. . . . Whether or not such programs can be described as "remedial," the message conveyed is that it is acceptable to harm a member of the group excluded from the benefit or privilege.**

Construction Contracts Revisited

In 1995, *Adarand Constructors, Inc. v. Peña* took a large step back from the Court's relaxed review standard in the *Metro Broadcasting* case. In the *Adarand Constructors* case, the Department of Transportation paid extra to prime contractors who subcontracted work to small businesses run by "socially and economically disadvantaged individuals." Companies run by minority groups automatically qualified for that status. Because of the preferences, guardrail work on a Colorado project went to Gonzales Construction Company instead of Adarand.

"[A]ll racial classifications, imposed by whatever federal, state, or local governmental actor, must be analyzed by a reviewing court under strict scrutiny," wrote Justice O'Connor. "In other words, such classifications are constitutional only

Affirmative Action

if they are narrowly tailored measures that further compelling government interests." The Court sent the case back for review under the stricter standard.

Justice Antonin Scalia's concurring opinion underscored his concern about the divisiveness of affirmative action preferences. And Justice Clarence Thomas argued that the affirmative action program's benign purpose did not shield it from strict scrutiny. "There can be no doubt that the paternalism that appears to lie at the heart of this program is at war with the principle of inherent equality that underlies and infuses our Constitution," he wrote.

On the other hand, Justice John Paul Stevens saw nothing wrong with having a more relaxed standard for reviewing programs meant to help disadvantaged groups. In his view, a decision to help a disadvantaged minority was "fundamentally different" from action to discriminate against them. Likewise, Justice Ruth Bader Ginsburg argued:

> **Congress surely can conclude that a carefully designed affirmative action program may help to realize, finally, the 'equal protection of the laws' the Fourteenth Amendment has promised since 1868.**

With the Court so divided, lawsuits kept challenging the validity of affirmative action programs. In 2003, the Supreme Court again looked at the question of affirmative action in university admissions.

The University of Michigan Cases

When the Supreme Court examined the University of Michigan's affirmative action policies in 2003, it again reached split decisions. In *Grutter* v. *Bollinger*, the Court upheld the University of Michigan Law School's policy of taking race and ethnicity into account as a factor in making admissions decisions. In *Gratz* v. *Bollinger*, however,

The Supreme Court and Affirmative Action

the Court held that the preferences for certain minority groups at the undergraduate College of Literature, Arts and Sciences (LAS) violated both the Constitution and federal civil rights laws.

The *Gratz* case was a class action in which named plaintiffs Jennifer Gratz and Patrick Hamacher sued on behalf of all students who did not get admitted from 1995 onward because LAS treated them less favorably than other racial or ethnic groups. During the relevant time, LAS scored applicants by awarding points based on their high school courses and grades, scores on either the SAT or ACT (American College Test), and other factors. Students with 100 to 150 points generally got in. Students scoring between 90 and 99 might have decisions postponed until later in the process and then might be admitted. Students scoring between 75 and 89 might be delayed until LAS saw which accepted students enrolled. Otherwise, they and any students scoring under 75 were rejected outright.

Significantly, a "miscellaneous" category in the scoring system awarded applicants twenty points just for being in an underrepresented ethnic or racial group. In contrast, personal achievement, leadership, or public service could win at most five points. An outstanding personal essay might earn an applicant just three points. In other words, one-fifth of the points needed for admission could come just from being a member of certain minority groups.

As a result, practically all minimally qualified applicants in those minority groups got in. If Jennifer and Patrick had been members of those minority groups, both would have gotten in under the point system. Because they were white, however, both were ultimately rejected.

A majority of the Court decided that automatically giving every underrepresented minority applicant an extra 20 points was "not narrowly tailored" to achieve the public university's interest in educational diversity. Yes, the university received thousands of applications each year. And yes, the

Affirmative Action

BARBARA GRUTTER WENT TO COURT TO CHALLENGE AFFIRMATIVE ACTION WHEN HER APPLICATION TO THE UNIVERSITY OF MICHIGAN LAW SCHOOL WAS REJECTED. THE SUPREME COURT REAFFIRMED THE LAW SCHOOL'S AFFIRMATIVE ACTION PROGRAM.

The Supreme Court and Affrmative Action

point system made life easier for the admissions office. However, the Court held, each applicant deserved to be considered as an individual apart from his or her race or ethnic group.

Indeed, Justice Thomas noted, the LAS policy not only discriminated against the disfavored ethnic groups. It also did not "sufficiently allow for the consideration of nonracial distinctions among underrepresented minority groups." Thus, it was unfair to applicants in both groups.

Dissenting Justices Stevens and Souter argued that neither Jennifer nor Patrick had standing to complain after they enrolled at other colleges. The majority, however, held that the fact that they had been discriminated against was grounds enough for them to challenge the school's policy.

Justice Ginsburg also argued that the Court should not use the same standard of review that would have applied to a policy meant to hurt minorities. "The stain of generations of racial oppression is still visible in our society, and the determination to hasten its removal remains vital," she wrote. Thus, she would have upheld the program.

In contrast to the undergraduate program, the law school's admission policy did not specify any automatic benefit for members of various minority groups. Instead, the extent to which race was a factor in decisions varied from case to case. The law school did not have any particular percentage or number of minorities it planned to admit. At the same time, however, it aimed to admit a "critical mass" of underrepresented minorities. This critical mass would be enough so that minority students would feel encouraged to participate in classes without feeling isolated.

For the year 2000, the law school admitted 35 percent of the applicants who were members of underrepresented minorities. Without any consideration of race, an expert for the law school testified, a color-blind admissions system would have admitted only one-tenth of those applicants. Instead of those minority groups making up just

Affirmative Action

under 15 percent of the class that enrolled, the expert estimated they would have made up only 4 percent.

The Court held that the law school's case-by-case policy satisfied the Constitution's requirements. Citing Justice Powell's opinion in the *Bakke* case, Justice Sandra Day O'Connor's majority opinion found that the university had a legitimate interest in ensuring diversity among its students:

> **We have long recognized that, given the important purpose of public education and the expansive freedoms of speech and thought associated with the university environment, universities occupy a special niche in our constitutional tradition. . . . Our conclusion that the Law School has a compelling interest in a diverse student body is informed by our view that attaining a diverse student body is at the heart of the Law School's proper institutional mission, and that "good faith" on the part of the university is "presumed" absent a showing to the contrary.**

Indeed, Justice O'Connor wrote, the benefits from having a diverse student body "are substantial." Diversity promotes cross-racial understanding and breaks down racial stereotypes. It also encourages more spirited and more interesting classroom discussions. Those benefits would help develop skills students need in the global marketplace.

Most importantly, the law school's admissions decisions involved "a highly individualized, holistic review of each applicant's file," regardless of race. "When using race as a 'plus' factor in university admissions, a university's admissions program must remain flexible enough to ensure that each applicant is evaluated as an individual and not in a way that makes an applicant's race or ethnicity the defining feature of his or her application," wrote O'Connor.

The Supreme Court and Affirmative Action

Last, but not least, O'Connor's majority opinion stressed the temporary nature of affirmative action:

> **Enshrining a permanent justification for racial preferences would offend this fundamental equal protection principle. We see no reason to exempt race-conscious admissions programs from the requirement that all governmental use of race must have a logical end point.**
>
> **. . . We expect that 25 years from now, the use of racial preferences will no longer be necessary to further the interest approved today.**

Justice Thomas's separate opinion disagreed with the majority's decision to uphold the law school policy. In his view, diversity should not be an end in itself.

Beyond that, Thomas saw no compelling public interest either in diversity or overly exclusive admissions policies. A university could not have low general admission standards but then impose higher requirements only on blacks. "Similarly," he wrote, "a university may not maintain a high admission standard and grant exemptions to favored races." The law school knew few blacks would meet its very high admission standards. Nonetheless, "Racial discrimination is not a permissible solution to the self-inflected wounds of this elitist admissions policy."

Justice Rehnquist argued that the law school's admissions policy was "simply a sham" to achieve racial balancing. The law school said its program was flexible. Yet, in practice, it resulted in "proportionate representation of applicants from selected minority groups." As support, Rehnquist showed the percentages of applicants from different ethnic groups for several years. Across the board, they were within a percentage point of the actual number admitted.

Getting to the Supreme Court

Relatively few cases on affirmative action get to the Supreme Court. In fact, most lawsuits are settled before they get to trial. And after courts rule on dispositive (final, case-ending) motions or parties have had a trial, the losers may not pursue all appeals. Even if they do, going all the way to the Supreme Court is still a long shot.

Parties can appeal a case to the Supreme Court from a United States Court of Appeals or their state's highest court. In very rare cases, the Supreme Court may also review a case from a federal district court. The Constitution also spells out a few instances where cases can start in the Supreme Court, such as lawsuits by one state against another.

About eight thousand requests for review come before the Supreme Court each year, mostly in a form called a petition for *certiorari*. Law clerks for the justices review those documents and prepare memoranda. After reviewing them, the justices vote. If four justices vote in favor of hearing a case, the Court issues an order granting *certiorari*.

The public importance of an issue is one factor that the Court considers. The Court is more likely to hear a case that will affect a large segment of the public than one that hinges on unique facts and circumstances. Lower courts' need for guidance also matters. For example, if two courts of appeals have issued conflicting decisions, the Court may accept a case in order to resolve the matter. Likewise, the Court may take a case if it feels the lower courts have incorrectly applied the ruling from an earlier Supreme Court case.

Presently, the Court hears and decides only about one hundred cases each year. Even then, the Court often hesitates on deciding constitutional questions. If a case can be decided on statutory grounds, the Court will usually do that instead of reaching for an opportunity to interpret the Constitution. Four of the justices took this approach in the *Bakke* case.

The Court will also decide an issue only in the context of an ongoing case and controversy. Put another way, the Court does not decide abstract issues. Thus, it dismissed a 1974 case on affirmative action in law school admissions, *DeFunis* v. *Odegaard*. A lower court had issued a temporary order directing the school to admit the plaintiff. By the time the case got before the Supreme Court, the plaintiff was about to graduate and the case was moot. In other words, the Court's ruling wouldn't have any real-world effect on the immediate parties, so it did not rule on the merits of DeFunis's challenges.

What happens to the appeals that the Supreme Court doesn't hear? The parties to those cases have already had at least one chance for appeal in either the state or federal court system. Thus, as a matter of due process, they have had their day in court. The last court's decision binds them. That decision also becomes a precedent for other cases that may come before that court.

Significantly, the Supreme Court's denial of *certiorari* is not a decision one way or the other on the merits of a case. Thus, the denial of *certiorari* does not serve as any precedent in the U.S. legal system. Any future decision on the issue will just have to wait for another case.

Affirmative Action

In Rehnquist's view, then, the policy was "tantamount to quotas." Yet a majority of the Court was willing to go along with it, as long as the law school did not say exactly what it was doing. As a result, universities would have little reason to make their admissions schemes "transparent and protective of individual review." In Rehnquist's view, that would ultimately prolong racial and ethnic hostilities.

Yet another problem stems from the Court's divided decisions. By upholding the law school's vague policy and overturning the very specific undergraduate policy, the Court seems almost to encourage government agencies and institutions to conduct any affirmative action programs in the shadows. Thus, the Court seems to be back at a point criticized by the pro-affirmative-action dissenters in *Bakke*: "[T]here is no basis for preferring a particular preference program simply because . . . it proceeds in a manner that is not immediately apparent to the public."

Ideally, a democratic government functions best when its actions are subject to public scrutiny. Regardless of its rulings on the specific programs, the Michigan cases seem to go against the goal of openness in America's democracy. The cases also guarantee that affirmative action will remain open for debate.

6
Moving Ahead

It's unclear just when the Supreme Court will rule again on affirmative action. By then, new justices may hold very different views from those who decided earlier cases. They might well urge the Court to diverge from some prior rulings.

In the meantime, lower courts will need to decide various issues. Under American law, lower courts must follow Supreme Court holdings. But Supreme Court opinions often leave room for different interpretations. And cases do not always fall clearly under the holding of one Supreme Court case or another.

Ongoing Legal Issues

As matters stand, the Supreme Court's rulings say no to quotas and other rigid or mechanical plans that give preferences based on nationality or sex. However, the Court's 2003 opinions said universities could consider race or

Affirmative Action

ethnicity as one of many factors in the admissions process. Just how far will this concept go?

The Michigan cases approved of schools aiming for a critical mass of minority students. That would mean enough numbers so that minority students would not feel awkward or intimidated in classes. But the Court gave no objective measure. Affirmative action critics might say that a small percentage should suffice. Yet some supporters might argue that the critical mass number could properly go all the way up to the percentage that a minority makes up in the general population.

Beyond this, some universities already appear racially and ethnically diverse when viewed as a whole. However, minorities may still be underrepresented in particular schools or fields of study. It's unclear how far courts will let institutions go in trying to build up diversity within specific sections of the university community.

For that matter, affirmative action for women remains a somewhat open question. Women make up a majority of the students at many undergraduate colleges. Yet they are still outnumbered by men in various science, math, and engineering majors, as well as in certain graduate fields.

Should schools, government agencies, or other sponsors be able to give women-only scholarships in certain areas? What about special girls' science and engineering camps or enrichment programs? Answers to these questions are unclear. Likewise, it's not clear whether schools can or should do anything to increase male enrollment in fields that were traditionally dominated by women, such as nursing or teaching.

Government agencies and private companies will face issues as well. The Michigan cases blessed universities' academic freedom to promote diversity as part of their educational mission. They hinted that diversity is also important for today's business world.

Moving Ahead

Private companies could argue that courts should accept their business judgment about what works best for meeting clients' needs in today's diverse markets. Critics, however, would recall early employment cases that held that client preferences could not excuse discrimination in the workplace. It's unclear which side would win.

Similarly, government agencies could argue that preferences in hiring or in contracting programs reflect a valid public purpose in promoting equality. Again, however, the Supreme Court cases are not clear on just how far they can go. At a minimum, agencies at the federal, state, and local level would probably need substantial factual support for why they have particular affirmative action programs.

Even then, people in the nonpreferred groups may well challenge programs. After all, a court may see affirmative action programs as making up a small part of the overall benefits from government employment or government contracting. To someone who was passed over, however, the issue can seem very substantial indeed.

For example, the Supreme Court dealt with minority contracting preferences in 1995 in *Adarand Constructors, Inc. v. Peña*. Afterward, various agencies continued affirmative action programs under revised guidelines. Generally, there are more limits now on presumptions that minority-owned businesses are disadvantaged. Nonminority firms also have more flexibility to qualify. Nonetheless, billions of federal contract dollars still flow through the Small Business Administration's (SBA's) programs for disadvantaged businesses. Without presumptions for minority-owned businesses, however, the SBA program would probably deal with far fewer contractors. Overall bidding opportunities for other firms would thus increase.

The issue is especially important for niche companies that specialize in a particular type of work. One recent challenge, for example, came from a nonminority Long

Affirmative Action

Island firm that specializes in helicopter flight simulators. Getting rid of minority preferences would leave it free to bid on more government work.

Ballot Battles and Percentage Plans

States that ended affirmative action have seen effects in their state universities. In California, for example, overall enrollment of some minorities may not have dropped. Nonetheless, minority enrollment went down at the state's more selective colleges and universities. At the University of California at Berkeley, for example, 260 students in the 1997 first-year class were African American. By 2004, however, only 108 black students enrolled in the first-year class—less than 3 percent of the total. The entering class for the university's engineering program had no black first-year students.

"This is a problem that has got to get solved," Berkeley's chancellor, Robert Birgeneau, announced. "We're not meeting our obligation as a public institution." In Birgeneau's view, Californians did not bargain for such results when they voted for Proposition 209.

For the University of California's overall first-year class in 2005, Asian Americans made up about 40 percent of the class. White students accounted for nearly 34 percent, while about 6 percent of the class was Hispanic. Blacks made up about 3 percent.

Resuming racial and ethnic preferences might increase black and Latino representation at elite colleges in California. However, that could come at the expense of other minorities that have also historically suffered significant discrimination in America. The National Center for Policy Analysis, for example, has argued that Proposition 209 actually increased opportunities for Asian Americans

Moving Ahead

STUDENTS AT THE UNIVERSITY OF CALIFORNIA BERKELEY PROTESTED THE REPEAL OF AFFIRMATIVE ACTION IN THE STATE IN 1997.

Affirmative Action

PAUL ROCKWELL, CHAIRMAN OF "ANGRY WHITE GUYS FOR AFFIRMATIVE ACTION," SPEAKS OUT AGAINST CALIFORNIA PROPOSITION 209, A 1996 BALLOT INITIATIVE THAT DISMANTLED AFFIRMATIVE ACTION PROGRAMS IN THE STATE.

Moving Ahead

at California's state universities. The group opposes affirmative action. Meanwhile, more states could pass their own ballot initiatives on affirmative action. If and when that happens, the proposals will likely face substantial opposition.

After the Supreme Court's 2003 rulings, for example, Ward Connerly and the Michigan Civil Rights Institute began a ballot campaign to outlaw affirmative action in Michigan. "Do we have so little confidence in the American spirit and in yet unborn Americans of African and Mexican descent that we consign them to another generation of presumed inadequacy?" Connerly asked in a speech at the University of Michigan. The issue was slated for the Michigan ballot in November 2006. Heated debates in other states will likely follow.

Meanwhile, governments, universities, and companies still struggle with ways to increase diversity and equal opportunity. Aside from outright preferences, schools may increase efforts in recruiting, outreach, and other types of programs that raise less controversy.

The future of race-neutral percentage plans is up in the air, too. The University of Texas began such a system after a court found its previous affirmative action policy unconstitutional. As of 2005, the plan promised public university admission to Texas residents graduating in the top tenth of their high school class.

By 2005, students admitted under that percentage plan made up nearly 70 percent of UT-Austin's incoming class. This left less discretion for admissions officers to admit students who did not make the initial cut, as well as fewer seats for attracting talented applicants from outside the state.

Percentage-plan critics question whether an applicant from a school with low academic performance overall

Affirmative Action

should win out over someone from the twelfth percentile at a prestigious high school. In light of that dilemma, the university may eventually go back to taking race and nationality into account, consistent with the Supreme Court's 2003 opinions. However, that solution would not resolve the continuing disparities among the states' schools.

California's public universities adopted their own percentage plan in 2001. Residents graduating in the top eighth of their high school classes get guaranteed admission to some school within the state's university system. However, some students may need to go to community college first. Florida's Talented Twenty Program was another variation on the approach.

Supporters say that percentage plans help increase diversity overall. Opponents argue that they merely disguise the problem of differences in groups' achievement. Either way, elite schools' admissions policies will continue to stimulate arguments on both sides of the affirmative action debate.

Toward Real Equal Opportunity

In 2003, Supreme Court Justice Sandra Day O'Connor predicted affirmative action would no longer be necessary twenty-five years from then. Is this realistic?

"Is it fair to say to a black parent: your child to be born eight years from now will still need a preference when he or she applies to college in the year 2028?" affirmative action critic Ward Connerly asked in a speech after the Court announced its 2003 decisions. As his work on various ballot initiatives shows, Connerly feels the time to end affirmative action is now.

Affirmative action supporters, on the other hand, wonder how much real progress American society will

Moving Ahead

An affirmative action supporter holds up a sign in protest of Ward Connerly's anti-affirmative action speech on the campus of the University of Michigan in Ann Arbor on July 8, 2003.

Affirmative Action

make in the next twenty-five years. As Martin Kurzweil explains:

> **Even with the most optimistic assumptions, the share of student bodies from minority backgrounds in 25 years would fall significantly short of the current share. It is certainly the goal of every supporter of affirmative action that there will eventually come a day when it will no longer be necessary—but the essentially random target of 25 years is simply unrealistic, by our best estimates.**

Ideally, the United States will make progress in improving opportunities for all its citizens, regardless of race, ethnic background, gender, or other factors. Getting to that point, however, presents significant challenges.

People of color can be found in all social and economic levels of American society. Yet they are still more likely than whites to live in areas with large concentrations of poverty. Statistically speaking, then, they are more likely to experience the social and economic problems that go along with that, including higher crime, more limited job opportunities, and poorer-quality schools.

Bringing schools up to par is a huge challenge. Making sure that all children get a basic, quality education is the goal of laws like 2002's No Child Left Behind Act. Among other things, public schools must show that students are in fact learning basic material, or the schools risk losing federal aid or other benefits. Because the law requires a solid basic education for all students, all students should have the opportunity to compete academically without regard to race or ethnicity.

However, many school districts do not have the resources they need to achieve those criteria. Schools may thus feel trapped in a Catch-22. They have to meet certain standards. But practical circumstances may make that impossible. And failure can mean further cutbacks in funds, so it becomes even harder to give children a good education.

Additionally, the law's emphasis on standardized testing means many schools spend lots of time "teaching to the test." As a result, they have less time for developing critical thinking, research methods, writing techniques, and other skills that young people need to succeed in college and in life.

Family structure is another area of concern. In general, children in two-parent homes are more likely to grow up with various economic advantages. Divorce hits people in all economic and ethnic groups. Yet researchers at the University of California, Davis, note black children often experience a much bigger drop in family income afterward than white children do: 53 percent versus 30 percent in the first two years. Partly this reflects the fact that more black women are already working when they get divorced, so they have less opportunity to make up the spouse's lost income.

Single-parenthood rates also differ among ethnic groups. Pregnancy rates and the frequency of sex outside of marriage may not differ all that much. Yet single women may view the fathers of their children as less attractive marriage candidates when socioeconomic factors significantly limit the men's opportunities. Thus, sociologist William Julius Wilson has argued that, because of a lack of jobs in inner cities and other factors, single black mothers often have less economic incentive to marry than single white mothers do.

This certainly does not mean that children cannot grow up well in single-parent homes. In fact, many young people do just that. Nor is it meant to pass judgment on any person's decision. One can argue strongly against

Affirmative Action

divorce or premarital sex, just as one can argue strongly that people should not stay in an unhappy marriage or get married simply because a pregnancy occurs.

Nonetheless, to the extent that children grow up without the socioeconomic benefits that living in a two-parent home may bring, that can limit their opportunities. And, unfortunately, this affects some ethnic groups more than others. In the long run, getting rid of the socioeconomic disparities between groups would help remove perceived barriers to marriage. Meanwhile, children in such circumstances may need additional resources to help put them on an equal footing, whatever their race may be.

All of this costs money. Some people feel that the ultimate answer lies in personal responsibility. In other words, it is up to individual parents to do whatever it takes to make sure their children have good opportunities in life. And it is up to young people to make the most of whatever situation they find themselves facing. Many people have overcome adversity, and there are no barriers preventing people who truly want a better life from pursuing it. Under this view, the more people expect of themselves, the more they are likely to achieve.

Other people say it is fine for adults to live with the consequences of their choices. However, children's chances for success in life should not depend on the accident of their race, ethnic group, gender, or other factors beyond their control. Under this view, government programs can and should make up for some of the disadvantages that poor children face, especially poor children of color.

Of course, money to pay for those social programs would need to come from somewhere else in the government budget, or from added taxes. Policy makers and voters may not be willing to make those choices.

Moving Ahead

Additionally, simply throwing money at a problem does not necessarily solve it. This is especially true when policy makers disagree about what the causes are. For example, educators have reported an "achievement gap" between how white and black students perform even in integrated, well-to-do school districts.

One explanation, suggests Terrence Pell at the Center for Individual Rights, is that students are responding to what is expected of them. Black students might feel a C grade is good enough, and affirmative action programs at the university level reinforce that belief. If society expects the same high performance from everyone, then students should eventually expect that from themselves.

On the other hand, black students may be working just as hard on homework and other school tasks. However, suggests Ronald Ferguson at Harvard University, they may be more likely to act tough to appear popular. This can influence how teachers view and respond to students, which can affect grades. Stereotype anxiety may also cause some students to perform poorly. In other words, students may perform poorly because they worry that others don't expect them to succeed. Peer pressure is often a factor, too.

In any case, there are no easy answers. But unless changes take place somewhere—either through government, the private sector, or individual initiative—the status quo is likely to continue. That situation is not likely to please either affirmative action's foes or its supporters.

Prejudice remains a problem in American society, too. The law treats women and people of color much better today than it did fifty years ago. However, the law is not self-enforcing, and many individuals continue to experience bigotry and discrimination. Stronger enforcement of civil rights laws can help. Greater willingness to speak out

Close-up on Cleveland's Minority Clerkship Program

As in most of the United States, minorities are still only a small percentage of the legal bar in Cleveland, Ohio. Just 6 percent of the area's associate attorneys were minorities in 2003. For over twelve years, the Cleveland Bar Association has worked to boost their representation with its Minority Clerkship Program.

Clerkships are summer jobs for law students at legal firms, government offices, or other organizations. Employers get help with research and writing projects, plus a chance to evaluate students for possible full-time jobs. Law students get valuable work experience and professional guidance as they develop professional contacts.

Though some firms hire only a few summer clerks, others hire a dozen or more. Under the bar association's clerkship program, more than twenty organizations agree to hire one first-year minority law student for the summer. Minority students must meet strict standards, including a graded writing assignment and interviews.

Summer clerks hired through the program get paid on the same basis as other summer clerks. Firms do not extend permanent employment offers at the end of the summer, though, so the program does not deprive anyone of a full-time job. Program participants can, however, go through firms' normal recruiting processes during their second and third years of law school.

"This gives first year law students an opportunity to build their resumes, so they can compete more effectively when they are second year students," says program director Donnie Long.

Meanwhile, the program gets law firms to seriously consider talented students they might otherwise overlook. Sometimes those strengths wouldn't normally stand out on résumés.

Among other things, minority law students are more likely than whites to be the first in their families to finish college and pursue an advanced degree. They are more likely to hold jobs while going to law school. Plus, they are more likely to have encountered prejudice.

"They're just knocking down barriers right and left," says Long. "That says a lot for determination and tenacity." Those qualities can help people become very good lawyers indeed.

Affirmative Action

AFFIRMATIVE ACTION AND CIVIL RIGHTS LAWS NOTWITHSTANDING, PREJUDICE REMAINS A FORCE IN AMERICAN LIFE. THE GRAND DRAGON OF THE MICHIGAN KU KLUX KLAN ADDRESSES THE CROWD AT A KKK RALLY IN AUGUST 1999 IN DOWNTOWN CLEVELAND, OHIO.

Moving Ahead

against offensive conduct can also shape societal norms. Sadly, however, this does not all happen overnight.

As long as racist and sexist attitudes continue, some people will try to violate other people's rights. That deprives people of real equal opportunity, and it deprives America of the full talents its people can contribute to society.

In *Grutter v. Bollinger*, Supreme Court Justice Ruth Bader Ginsburg wrote:

> **From today's vantage point, one may hope, but not firmly forecast, that over the next generation's span, progress toward nondiscrimination and genuinely equal opportunity will make it safe to sunset affirmative action.**

You are part of that next generation. Your views and your actions on civil rights issues will help decide the future of the United States.

Notes

Chapter 1

p. 7, Michael Levenson, "BC Coach Alleges Gender Bias at BU," *Boston Globe*, July 5, 2005, p. B6.

pp. 7–8, *Taxman v. Board of Education of the Township of Piscataway*, 91 F.3d 1547 (1995), cert. granted, 521 U.S. 117, and dismissed, 522 U.S. 1010 (1997). *See also* Michael Booth, "Teacher's Libel Suit Rejected in Aftermath of Taxman Race Case," *The Legal Intelligencer*, July 25, 2001, p. 4.

pp. 8–9, Center for Individual Rights, "*Tompkins v. Alabama State University*," September 22, 2004. http://www.cirusa.org/cases/tompkins_v_alabama.html (accessed August 8, 2005). *See also* "News Briefs," *Birmingham News*, April 3, 1997, p. 3B; Kent Faulk and Mary Orndorff, "ASU, A&M Go All Out To Draw White Students," *Birmingham News*, August 22, 1996, p. 3B.

Notes

p. 9, "White Police Officer Wins Reverse Bias Suit," *Houston Chronicle*, April 19, 2002, p. A19.

pp. 13–14, Pamela Paul, "A Question of Quotas," *American Demographics*, May 1, 2003 (accessed through InfoTrac OneFile, August 6, 2005); Tim B. Heaton, Bruce A. Chadwick, and Cardell K. Jacobson, *Statistical Handbook on Racial Groups in the United States* (Phoenix, AZ: Oryx Press, 2000), p. 332; Richard Morin, "Misperceptions Cloud Whites' View of Blacks," *Washington Post*, July 11, 2001, p. A1; Alice O'Connor, Chris Tilly, and Lawrence Bobo, eds. *Urban Inequality: Evidence from Four Cities* (New York: Russell Sage Foundation, 2001), pp. 165–C169. See generally *The Washington Post/Kaiser Family Foundation/Harvard University Survey Project*, "Race and Ethnicity in 2001: Attitudes, Perceptions, and Experiences," August 2001. http://www.kff.org/kaiserpolls/upload/Race-and-Ethnicity-in-2001-Attitudes-Perceptions-and-Experiences-Toplines-Survey.pdf (accessed December 4, 2005).

pp. 15–17, U.S. Census Bureau, Statistical Abstract of the United States, 2004–2005, pp. 14, 18. http://www.census.gov/prod/2004pubs/04statab/pop.pdf (accessed August 6, 2005). U.S. Census Bureau, "Projected Population of the United States, by Race and Hispanic Origin: 2000 to 2050," March 18, 2004. http://www.census.gov/ipc/www/usinterimproj/natprojtab01a.pdf (accessed August 6, 2005).

p. 16, Gwen Filosa, "Fired White Workers Are Awarded $1.9 Million," *Times-Picayune* (New Orleans), March 31, 2005, p. 1; Adam Nossiter, "Orleans Race Bias Case Goes to Jury," *Associated Press* State & Local Wire, March 29, 2005 (accessed through Lexis-Nexis Academic Universe, March 29, 2005). *See also* Rebecca Mowbray, "New Orleans DA in Political Bat-

Affirmative Action

tle," *Boston Globe*, March 27, 2005, p. A15; Adam Nossiter, "New Orleans Prosecutor Defends Firings in Race Bias Suit," *Associated Press* State & Local Wire, March 18, 2005 (accessed through LexisNexis Academic Universe, March 29, 2005); Joan Treadway, "Fired Workers Say Qualifications Ignored," *Times-Picayune*, March 10, 2005, Metro, p. 1; Gwen Filosa, "Jordan's Race Bias Trial Set To Begin," *Times-Picayune*, March 8, 2005, Metro, p. 1; "New Orleans DA Sued Over Mass Firings," *Associated Press* State & Local Wire, May 31, 2003 (accessed through LexisNexis Academic Universe, March 19, 2005).

Chapter 2

pp. 23–24, Civil Rights Cases, 109 U.S. 3, 25 (1883).

p. 24, *Plessy v. Ferguson*, 163 U.S. 537, 559 (1896).

pp. 24–25, *Brown v. Board of Education*, 347 U.S. 483 (1954).

p. 25, "Feminism Reborn," DigitalHistory.com, 2004. http://www.digitalhistory.uh.edu/database/article_display.cfm?HHID=380 (accessed July 13, 2005).

p. 26, Karen Blumenthal, "Title IX's Next Hurdle," *Wall Street Journal*, July 6, 2005, pp. B1–B2.

pp. 26–27, John F. Kennedy, Executive Order 10925, March 6, 1961, published at 26 Fed. Reg. 1977 (March 8, 1961).

p. 27, Lyndon B. Johnson, Executive Order 11246, September 24, 1965, published at 30 Fed. Reg. 12319 (September 28, 1965); Lyndon B. Johnson, Executive Order 11375, October 13, 1967, published at 32 Fed. Reg. 14303 (October 17, 1967). *See also* Rachel Kranz, *Affirmative Action* (New York: Facts on File, 2002), p. 15.

pp. 27–28, Kranz, *Affirmative Action*, pp. 16–17; Dennis Doverspike, Mary Anne Taylor, and Winfred Arthur Jr., *Affirmative Action: A Psychological Perspective* (Huntington, NY: Nova Science Publishers, Inc., 2000), p. 9;

Notes

"Affirmative Action: History and Rationale," from *Affirmative Action Review: Report to the President*, Chapter 2, July 19, 1995. http://clinton4.nara.gov/WH/EOP/OP/html/aa/aa02.html (accessed July 13, 2005).

p. 28, Charles V. Dale, *Affirmative Action Revisited*. New York: Novinka Books, 2002), pp. 11–15. *See* Pennsylvania Advisory Committee to the U.S. Commission on Civil Rights, "Barriers Facing Minority- and Women-Owned Businesses in Pennsylvania," August 2002, p. x. http://www.usccr.gov/pubs/sac/pa0802/pa0802.pdf (accessed July 14, 2005).

p. 30, Bob Laird, *The Case for Affirmative Action in University Admissions* (Berkeley, CA: Bay Tree publishing, 2005), p. 1; William G. Bowen and Derek Bok, *The Shape of the River: Long-Term Consequences of Considering Race in College and University Admissions* (Princeton: Princeton University Press, 1998), p. 4.

p. 30, James L. Curtis, *Affirmative Action in Medicine* (Ann Arbor: University of Michigan Press, 2003), p. 1.

p. 31, *Regents of the University of California v. Bakke*, 438 U.S. 265 (1978).

p. 31, *Steelworkers v. Weber*, 443 U.S. 193 (1979).

p. 31, *Fullilove v. Klutznick*, 448 U.S. 448 (1980).

p. 31, *Johnson v. Transportation Agency*, 480 U.S. 616 (1987); *United States v. Paradise*, 480 U.S. 149 (1987).

pp. 31, 34, *City of Richmond v. Croson*, 488 U.S. 469 (1989). *See also* John Fobanjong, *Understanding the Backlash Against Affirmative Action* (Huntington, NY: Nova Science Publishers, 2001), pp. 34–36.

pp. 32–33, "President Lyndon B. Johnson's Commencement Address at Howard University: 'To Fulfill These Rights,'" June 4, 1965, Lyndon Baines Johnson Library and Museum, 2002. http://www.lbjlib.utexas.edu/johnson/archives.hom/speeches.hom/650604.asp (accessed July 13, 2005).

p. 34, *Maryland State Troopers Association v. Evans*, 993

Affirmative Action

F.2d 1072 (4th Cir. 1993); *Detroit Police Officers Association* v. *Young*, 989 F.2d 225 (6th Cir. 1993).

p. 34, *Adarand Constructors, Inc.* v. *Peña*, 515 U.S. 200 (1995).

p. 34, White House Office of the Press Secretary, Statement by the President, June 13, 1995. http://www.inform.umd.edu/EdRes/Topic/Diversity/Response/Action/pres (accessed July 14, 2005). See Charles V. Dale, *Affirmative Action Revisited* (New York: Novinka Books, 2002), pp. 34–35; Infoplease, "Affirmative Action Setbacks: 1997 News of the Nation," Pearson Education, 2005. http://www.infoplease.com/ipa/A0194236.html (accessed July 14, 2005).

p. 35, *Hopwood* v. *Texas*, 78 F.3d 932 (5th Cir., 1996).

pp. 35–36, John Fobanjong, *Understanding the Backlash Against Affirmative Action* (Huntington, NY: Nova Science Publishers, 2001), pp. 172–174. *See also* Laird, *The Case for Affirmative Action in University Admissions*, pp. 37–41; Doverspike, Taylor, and Arthur, *Affirmative Action: A Psychological Perspective*, p. 12.

Chapter 3

p. 39, Patricia Gurin, et al., *Defending Diversity: Affirmative Action at the University of Michigan* (Ann Arbor: University of Michigan Press, 2004), pp. 99–100, 109.

p. 39, Martin Kurzweil, e-mail communication to author, August 4, 2005.

p. 40, Gurin et al., p. 107; Larry D. Roper, "Do Students Support Diversity Programs?" *Change*, November–December 2004, p. 48.

p. 41, "The 30 Best Companies for Diversity: How We Chose the 30 Best Companies for Diversity," *Black Enterprise*, July 2005, p. 118; Claudia H. Deutsch, "Bedrock of Law on Workplace Should Remain as Justice Exits," *New York Times*, July 4, 2005, p. 1; Tom McGhee, "Coors Scores Points on Diversity List," *Denver Post*, June 15, 2005, p. C2.

Notes

p. 41, James L. Curtis, *Affirmative Action in Medicine* (Ann Arbor: University of Michigan Press, 2003), pp. 1–2.

pp. 41–42, President Clinton's Remarks on Affirmative Action, National Archives, Washington, D.C., July 19, 1995. http://www.americanreview.us/affirm1.htm (accessed July 14, 2005). *See also* Rachel Kranz, *Affirmative Action* (New York: Facts on File, 2002), p. 121.

p. 42, DeWayne Wickham, "Photo Prank Using Leash Stirs Chilling Memories," *USA Today*, May 23, 2005, p. 11A; Andrea Weigl, "Jury Finds Bias in Noose Incident," *News & Observer* (Raleigh, NC), May 19, 2005, p. B1.

p. 43, Athena S. Cheng, "Affirmative Action for the Female Entrepreneur: Gender as a Presumed Socially Disadvantaged Group for 8(a) Program Purposes," *American University Journal of Gender, Social Policy and Law*, 2001, pp. 185, 219–221; Rebecca L. Berkeley, "Gender Based Affirmative Action: A Journey That Has Only Just Begun," *Washington University Journal of Urban and Contemporary Law*, Fall 1996, pp. 353, 363–366.

p. 43, Amanda Ripley, "Who Says a Woman Can't Be Einstein?" *Time*, March 7, 2005, p. 50. *See also* Marcella Bombardieri, "Harvard Appoints Professor to Senior Diversity Post," *Boston Globe*, July 21, 2005, p. B4; Marcella Bombardieri, "Summers Sets $50M Women's Initiative," *Boston Globe*, May 17, 2005, p. A1; Elizabeth Mehren, "Faculty Group Votes Lack of Confidence in Harvard Chief," *Los Angeles Times*, March 16, 2005, p. 1; "More Response to Remarks by Harvard Press," *Women in Higher Education*, March 2005, p. 3.

p. 45, Bob Laird, *The Case for Affirmative Action in University Admissions* (Berkeley, CA: Bay Tree Publications, 2005), p. 103.

p. 45, Shankar Vedantam, "See No Bias," *Washington Post*, January 23, 2005, p. W12; Jerry Kang, "Trojan

Affirmative Action

Horses of Race," *Harvard Law Review*, March 2005, pp. 1489, 1512; Sherry Williams, "'Black' Names Seen as Stigmatizing, Studies Find," *Columbus Dispatch*, June 5, 2005, p. 1I.

p. 46, Jaime M. Grant, "Affirmative Inaction," *NWSA Journal*, Fall 1998, p. 192.

p. 46, *Grutter v. Bollinger*, 539 U.S. 306, 345 (2003) (Ginsberg, J., concurring).

p. 46, Christopher Edley, Jr., *Not All Black and White: Affirmative Action and American Values* (New York: Hill and Wang, 1996), pp. 84–85.

p. 47, Bob Egelko, "Judge Defends Writing on Affirmative Action," *San Francisco Chronicle*, June 8, 2005, p. A4.

p. 47, William G. Bowen, "Stand and Prosper! Race and American Higher Education," address at University of Virginia, April 13, 2004. http://www.mellon.org/standandprosper.pdf (accessed August 19, 2005).

p. 47, *Regents of the University of California v. Bakke*, 438 U.S. 265, 395–396 (Marshall, J., dissenting).

pp. 47–48, United States Census Bureau, "Income, Poverty, and Health Insurance Coverage in the United States: 2003," Current Population Reports P60–226, August 2004, pp. 4, 41–44. http://www.census.gov/prod/2004pubs/p60226.pdf (accessed June 6, 2005). See also Fred L. Pincus, *Reverse Discrimination: Dismantling the Myth* (Boulder, CO: Lynne Rienner Publishers, 2003), pp. 13–14, 16.

p. 48, Shawna Orzechowski and Peter Sepielli, "Net Worth and Asset Ownership of Households: 1998 and 2000," U.S. Census Bureau Current Population Reports P70–88, May 2003, p. 14. http://www.census.gov/prod/2003pubs/p70–88.pdf(accessed June 6, 2005).

p . 48, United States Census Bureau, "Income, Poverty, and Health Insurance Coverage in the United States: 2003," pp. 5–6; Fobanjong, *Understanding the Backlash against Affirmative Action*, p. 54.

p. 49, FairTest, "2004 College Bound Seniors Test Scores:

Notes

SAT," undated. http://www.fairtest.org/nattest/SAT%20 Scoresn%202004%20Chart.pdf (accessed June 6, 2005); William G. Bowen, Martin A. Kurzweil, and Eugene M. Tobin, "A Thumb on the Scale," *Harvard Magazine*, May-June 2005, pp. 48, 50.

p. 49, Bob Laird, *The Case for Affirmative Action in University Admissions*, pp. 9–12.

p. 50, Fred L. Pincus, *Reverse Discrimination: Dismantling the Myth*, p. 17.

pp. 50–51, Tim J. Wise, *Affirmative Action: Racial Preference in Black and White* (New York: Routledge, 2005), pp. 29–33.

p. 51, Robert Wagmiller, "Race, Suburbanization, and the Spatial Segregation of Jobless Men," paper presented at American Sociological Society, August 2005; "Black Joblessness Blamed on Spatial Segregation," University at Buffalo press release, August 15, 2005.

p. 51, Wise, *Affirmative Action: Racial Preference in Black and White*, p. 34.

p. 51, Oyez U.S. Supreme Court Multimedia, "Sandra Day O'Connor," 2005. http://www.oyez.org/oyez/resource/legal_entity/102/print (accessed October 26, 2005). *See also* Jaime M. Grant, "Affirmative Inaction," *NWSA Journal*, Fall 1998, p. 192.

p. 52, 515 U.S. 200, 264, 269 (Souter, J., dissenting).

pp. 52–53, H. George Frederickson, "Public Administration and Social Equity," in Walter D. Broadnax, ed., *Diversity and Affirmative Action in Public Service* (Boulder, CO: Westview Press, 2000), pp. 5–20.

p. 53, Bob Laird, *The Case for Affirmative Action in University Admissions*, p. 104.

p. 53, Bowen, "Stand and Prosper! Race and American Higher Education."

pp. 54–55, Kurzweil, e-mail communication to author, August 4, 2005; Bowen, "Stand and Prosper! Race and American High Education." *See generally* William G.

Affirmative Action

Bowen, Martin A. Kurzweil, and Eugene M. Tobin, *Equity and Excellence in American Higher Education* (Charlottesville: University of Virginia Press, 2005).

p. 56, William G. Bowen and Derek Bok, *The Shape of the River: Long-term Consequences of Considering Race in College and University Admissions* (Princeton, NJ: Princeton University Press, 1998), pp. 43, 50–51.

p. 56, Elizabeth S. Anderson, "Racial Integration as a Compelling Interest," *Constitutional Commentary*, Spring 2004, p. 15.

pp. 56–57, Susan Sturm and Lani Guinier, "The Future of Affirmative Action," in Lani Guinier and Susan Sturm, *Who's Qualified?* (Boston: Beacon Press, 2001), pp. 4–7.

p. 58, *Gratz v. Bollinger*, 539 U.S. 244, 298, 304 (2003) (Ginsberg, J., dissenting).

p. 58, Bowen, Kurzweil, and Tobin, "A Thumb on the Scale," *Harvard Magazine*, May-June 2005, pp. 48, 50. See generally Bowen, Kurzweil, and Tobin, *Equity and Excellence in American Higher Education*.

Chapter 4

p. 60, *Plessy v. Ferguson*, 163 U.S. 537, 559-60 (1896) (Harlan, J., dissenting), cited in *Metro Broadcasting, Inc. v. FCC*, 497 U.S. 547, 631, 637 (Kennedy, J., dissenting) (1990), and *Hi-Voltage Wire Works, Inc. v. City of San Jose*, 12 P.3d 1068, 1073 (Cal. S.Ct., 2000). See *Brown v. Board of Education*, 347 U.S. 483, 494 (1954). See also *Gayle v. Browder*, 352 U.S. 903 (1956).

p. 61, *Metro Broadcasting, Inc., v. FCC*, 497 U.S. 547, 635 (1990) (Kennedy, J., dissenting).

p. 61, *Adarand Constructors, Inc. v. Peña*, 515 U.S. 200, 239 (1995) (Scalia, J., concurring).

p. 61, *City of Richmond v. Croson*, 488 U.S. 469, 493 (1989).

Notes

p. 61, 488 U.S. 469, 516-17 (1989) (Stevens, J.).

p. 62, 488 U.S. 469, 527-28 (Scalia, J., concurring).

p. 63, *DeFunis* v. *Odegaard*, 416 U.S. 312, 337 (1974) (Douglas, J., dissenting), quoted in *City of Richmond v. J. A. Croson Co.*, 488 U.S. 469, 527 (Scalia, J., concurring).

p. 68, Larry Elder, *The Ten Things You Can't Say in America* (New York: St. Martin's Griffin, 2000), pp. 45–47.

p. 68, Richard H. Sander, "A Systemic Analysis of Affirmative Action in American Law Schools," *Stanford Law Review*, November 2004, p. 367. See also Richard Sander, "A Reply to Critics," *Stanford Law Review*, May 2005, p. 1963.

p. 68, Pat Wingert, "Affirmative Action: Making the Grade?" *Newsweek*, January 31, 2005, p. 7. See also Kevin Carey, "A Matter of Degrees: Improving Graduation Rates in Four-Year Colleges and Universities," May 2004. http://www2.edtrust.org/NR/rdonlyres/11B4283F-104E-4511-B0CA-1D3023231157/0/highered.pdf (accessed June 30, 2005).

pp. 68–69, Terrence Pell, telephone interview with author, July 25, 2005.

p. 69, Elder, *The Ten Things You Can't Say in America*, p. 115.

pp. 69–70, "Remarks by Ward Connerly, Chairman, American Civil Rights Institute," March 23, 2000. http://www.acri.org/spchbkrvw/mar23.html (accessed June 14, 2005).

p. 70, *Adarand Constructors, Inc.* v. *Peña*, 515 U.S. 200, 240-41 (1995) (Thomas, J., concurring) (footnote omitted).

p. 71, Pell, telephone interview with author, July 25, 2005.

p. 71, Christopher B. Swanson, "Keeping Count and Losing Count: Calculating Graduation Rates for All Students under NCLB Accountability," Urban Institute, 2004, pp. iii, 27. http://www.urban.org/UploadedPDF/410843_

Affirmative Action

keeping_count.pdf (accessed June 30, 2005).

p. 72, Pell, telephone interview with author, July 25, 2005.

p. 73, U.S. Census Bureau, "Income, Poverty, and Health Insurance Coverage in the United States: 2003," Current Population Reports P60–226, August 2004, pp. 10, 28–32 http://www.census.gov/prod/2004pubs/p60-226.pdf (accessed June 6, 2005).

p. 73, Rod Watson, "Lack of Money Is the Root of the Grad Gap," *Buffalo News*, May 19, 2005, p. B1.

p. 74, Center for Individual Rights, "*Worth v. Jackson*," November 2, 2004. http://www.cir-usa.org/ cases/worth_v_martinez.html (accessed July 24, 2005). See also *Worth v. Jackson*, Case No. 02-1576 (RBW), 2005 U.S. Dist. LEXIS (D.D.C., July 19, 2005).

p. 75, *DeFunis v. Odegaard*, 416 U.S. 312, 342 (1974) (Douglas, J., dissenting).

p. 76, Pell, telephone interview with author, July 25, 2005. *See also* Greg Stohr, *A Black and White Case: How Affirmative Action Survived Its Greatest Legal Challenge* (Princeton, NJ: Bloomberg Press, 2004), pp. 45–49.

Chapter 5

pp. 78–80, *Regents of the University of California v. Bakke*, 438 U.S. 265 (1978).

pp. 80–81, *Steelworkers v. Weber*, 443 U.S. 193, 208-09 (1979) (citations omitted).

pp. 81–82, *Fullilove v. Klutznick*, 448 U.S. 448, 459, 481-85 (1980) (citations omitted).

p. 82, 448 U.S. at 495, 514-15 (Powell, J., concurring).

p. 82, 448 U.S. at 517, 523 (Marshall, J., concurring).

p. 82, 448 U.S. at 532, 539, 552-54 (Stevens, J., dissenting).

p. 82, *United States v. Paradise*, 480 U.S. 149 (1987).

pp. 82–83, *Johnson v. Transportation Agency*, 480 U.S. 616, 638 (1987).

pp. 83–84, *City of Richmond v. Croson*, 488 U.S. 469, 490, 493-494, 499 (1989).

Notes

- p. 84, 488 U.S. at 520, 524, 527–528 (Scalia, J., concurring), quoting from Bickel, *The Morality of Consent* (New Haven, CT: Yale University Press, 1977), p. 133.
- pp. 84–85, 488 U.S. at 528-29, 541 (Marshall, J., dissenting).
- p. 85, 488 U.S. at 561 (Blackmun, J., dissenting).
- p. 85, *Jett* v. *Dallas Independent School District*, 491 U.S. 701 (1989); *Patterson* v. *McClean Credit Union*, 491 U.S. 164 (1989); *Lorance* v. *AT&T Technologies*, 490 U.S. 900 (1989); *Martin* v. *Wilks*, 490 U.S. 755 (1989); *Wards Cove Packing* v. *Antonio*, 490 U.S. 642 (1989). See John Fobanjong, *Understanding the Backlash Against Affirmative Action* (Huntington, NY: Nova Science Publishers, 2001), pp. 32–33.
- pp. 85–86, *Metro Broadcasting, Inc.* v. *FCC*, 497 U.S. 547, 565-68, 597 (1990), quoting from H.R. Conf. Rep. No. 97–765, p. 43 (1982).
- pp. 86–87, 497 U.S. at 602, 609 (O'Connor, J., dissenting) (citations omitted).
- p. 87, 497 U.S. at 637 (footnote and citations omitted).
- pp. 87–88, *Adarand Constructors, Inc.* v. *Peña*, 515 U.S. 200, 235 (1995).
- p. 88, 515 U.S. at 240 (Thomas, J., concurring).
- p. 88, 515 U.S. at 247 (Stevens, J., dissenting).
- p. 88, 515 U.S. at 274 (Ginsberg, J., dissenting).
- pp. 88–89, *Grutter* v. *Bollinger*, 539 U.S. 306 (2003); *Gratz* v. *Bollinger*, 539 U.S. 244 (2003).
- pp. 89–91, *Gratz* v. *Bollinger*, 539 U.S. 244, 254–257, 270.
- p. 91, 539 U.S. 244, 281 (Thomas, J., concurring).
- p. 91, 539 U.S. 244, 298, 303-04 (Ginsberg, J., dissenting) (citations omitted).
- pp. 91–93, *Grutter* v. *Bollinger*, 539 U.S. 306, 330–333, 336–337, 342–343 (2003).

Affirmative Action

p. 93, 539 U.S. 306, 349, 350, 355 (Thomas, J., concurring in part and dissenting in part).

pp. 93–96, 539 U.S. 306, 378, 383, 385-386 (Rehnquist, J., dissenting) (citations omitted).

p. 94, *Regents of the University of California v. Bakke*, 438 U.S. 265 (1978).

p. 95, *DeFunis v. Odegaard*, 416 U.S. 312 (1974).

p. 96, *Regents of the University of California v. Bakke*, 438 U.S. 265, 379 (1978) (Brennan, J., dissenting in part).

Chapter 6

p. 99, *Adarand Constructors, Inc. v. Peña*, 515 U.S. 200 (1995).

pp. 99–100, Eric Wolff, "Frustrated, Long Island Contractor Attacks Federal 'Set Aside' Program," *New York Sun*, July 7, 2003, p. 11; Center for Individual Rights, "*Dynalantic v. Department of Defense*," September 22, 2004. http://www.cir-usa.org/cases/dynalantic_v_dod.html (accessed August 8, 2005).

p. 100, "Berkeley Chancellor Vows To Increase Minority Enrollment," *Black Issues in Higher Education*, May 5, 2005, p. 8.

pp. 100–103, Rebecca Trounson, "UC Is Unbiased in Admissions, Analysis Finds," *Los Angeles Times*, July 22, 2005, p. B6; National Center for Policy Analysis, "Affirmative Action: Without Preferences, Asian Americans Gain Admission," 2001. http://www.ncpa.org/pd/affirm/pdaa/pdaa34.html (accessed December 7, 2005).

p. 103, Ward Connerly, "Taking It to Michigan," *National Review Online*, July 8, 2003. http://www.nationalreview.com/comment/comment-connerly070803.asp (accessed August 9, 2005). See *Michigan Civil Rights Initiative v. Board of State Canvassers*, Michigan Court of Appeals, Case No. 264204, 2005 Mich. App. LEXIS 2677 (October 31, 2005).

pp. 103–104, Carlos Guerra, "Top Ten Percent Rule Woes Highlight Need for Equality in Education," *San Antonio Express-News*, June 21, 2005, p. 1B; Bob Laird, *The Case for Affirmative Action in University Admissions* (Berkeley, CA: Bay Tree Publishing, 2005), p. 31.

p. 104, "UC's New Admissions Policy Expected To Increase Minority Enrollment," *Black Issues in Higher Education*, August 16, 2001, p. 12.

p. 104, Ward Connerly, "Taking It to Michigan."

p. 106, Martin Kurzweil, e-mail communication with author, August 4, 2005.

p. 106, No Child Left Behind Act, P.L. 107-110 (2002). *See generally* "No Child Left Behind," ED.gov, 2005 http://www.ed.gov/nclb/overview/intro/edpicks.jhtml?src=ln (accessed June 20, 2005).

p. 107, UC Davis News Service, "Divorce and Marriage Affect Black Children More," May 25, 2005. http://www.news.ucdavis.edu/search/news_detail.lasso?id=7376 (accessed August 9, 2005).

p. 107, *See*, e.g., Renate Forste, "Prelude to Marriage or Alternative to Marriage? A Social Demographic Look at Cohabitation in the U.S.," *Journal of Law & Family Studies*, 2002, pp. 91, 95–97; Parvin R. Huda, "Singled Out: A Critique of the Representation of Single Motherhood in Welfare Discourse," *William and Mary Journal of Women and the Law*, Winter 2001, pp. 341, 372–374; Jill Duerr Berrick, *Faces of Poverty: Portraits of Women and Children on Welfare* (New York: Oxford University Press, 1995), p. 174, n55.

p. 109, Lynette Clemetson, "Trying to Close the Achievement Gap," *Newsweek*, June 7, 1999, p. 36.

p. 109, Terrence Pell, telephone interview with author, July 25, 2005.

Affirmative Action

p. 109, Michael Sadowski, "Closing the Gap One School at a Time," *Harvard Education Letter*, May/June 2001. http://www.edletter.org/past/issues/2001mj/gap.shtml (accessed August 22, 2005). *See also* Michael A. Fletcher, "A Good-School, Bad-Grade Mystery," *Washington Post*, Friday, October 23, 1998, p. A1.

pp. 110–111, Donnie Long, telephone interview with author, June 16, 2005. *See also* D. Larkin Chernault, "Why We Can't Wait," *Cleveland Bar Journal*, February 2005, p. 4.

p. 113, *Grutter* v. *Bollinger*, 539 U.S. 306, 346 (Ginsberg, J., concurring).

Further Information

Further Reading

Grapes, Brian J., ed. *Affirmative Action*. San Diego: Greenhaven Press, 2000.

Maltz, Leora. *Affirmative Action*. Farmington Hills, MI: Greenhaven Press, 2005.

Marzilli, Alan. *Affirmative Action*. Philadelphia: Chelsea House Publishers, 2004.

McPherson, Stephanie. *The Bakke Case and the Affirmative Action Debate*. Berkeley Heights, NJ: Enslow Publishers, 2005.

Stefoff, Rebecca. *The Bakke Case: Challenge to Affirmative Action*. New York: Marshall Cavendish Benchmark, 2006.

Williams, Mary E., ed. *Discrimination*. San Diego: Greenhaven Press, 2003.

Affirmative Action

Organizations and Web Sites

Adversity.Net
P.O. Box 7099, Silver Spring, MD 20907
301.588.0778
http://www.adversity.net

American Association for Affirmative Action
888 16th Street, NW, Suite 800, Washington, DC 20006
800.252.8952
http://www.affirmativeaction.org

American Civil Liberties Union
125 Broad Street, New York, NY 10004
212.549.2500
http://www.aclu.org

Center for Equal Opportunity
14 Pidgeon Hill Drive, Suite 500, Sterling, VA 20165
703.421.5443
http://ceousa.org

Center for Individual Rights
1233 20th Street, NW, Suite 300, Washington, DC 20036
877.426.2665
http://www.cir-usa.org

Coalition to Defend Affirmative Action, Integration & Immigration Rights and Fight for Equality By Any Means Necessary (BAMN)
P.O. Box 24834, Detroit, MI 48224
313.468.3398
http://www.bamn.com

Further Information

National Association for the Advancement of
Colored People
4805 Mt. Hope Drive, Baltimore, MD 21215
877.622.2798
http://naacp.org

U.S. Department of Labor
200 Constitution Avenue, NW, Washington, DC 20210
866.487.2365
http://www.dol.gov
http://www.dol.gov/dol/topic/hiring/affirmativeact.htm

U.S. Equal Employment Opportunity Commission
1801 L Street, NW, Washington, DC 20507
202.663.4900
http://www.eeoc.gov

Bibliography

Antonio, A.L., et al. "Effects of Racial Diversity on Complex Thinking in College Students." *Psychological Science*, August 2004, pp. 507–510.

Ball, Howard. *The Bakke Case: Race, Education, and Affirmative Action*. Lawrence: University Press of Kansas, 2000.

Bertrand, Marianne, and Sendhill Mullainathan. "Are Emily and Brendan More Employable than Lakisha and Jamal? A Field Experiment on Labor Market Discrimination." November 18, 2002. http://gsb.uchicago.edu/pdf/bertrand.pdf (accessed May 11, 2005).

Bhattacharjee, Yudhijit. "No Meeting of the Minds on Women Faculty." *Science*, October 15, 2004, p. 389.

Bowen, William G., Martin A. Kurzweil, and Eugene M. Tobin. *Equity and Excellence in American Higher Education*. Charlottesville: University of Virginia Press, 2005.

Bibliography

Broadnax, Walter D., ed. *Diversity and Affirmative Action in Public Service*. Boulder, CO: Westview Press, 2000.

Chavez, Lydia. *The Color Bind: California's Battle To End Affirmative Action*. Berkeley: University of California Press, 1998.

Curtis, James L. *Affirmative Action in Medicine: Improving Health Care for Everyone*. Ann Arbor: University of Michigan Press, 2003.

Dale, Charles V. *Affirmative Action Revisited*. New York: Novinka Books, 2002.

Doverspike, Dennis, Mary Anne Taylor, and Winfried Arthur, Jr. *Affirmative Action: A Psychological Perspective*. Huntington, NY: Nova Science Publishers, Inc., 2000.

Edley, Christopher, Jr. *Not All Black and White: Affirmative Action and American Values*. New York: Hill and Wang, 1996.

Fobanjong, John. *Understanding the Backlash Against Affirmative Action*. Huntington, NY: Nova Science Publishers, 2001.

Fried, Charles. "Courting Confusion." *New York Times*, October 21, 2004, p. A29.

Goldman, Alan H. *Justice and Reverse Discrimination*. Princeton, NJ: Princeton University Press, 1979.

Guinier, Lani, and Susan Sturm. *Who's Qualified?* Boston: Beacon Press, 2001.

Gurin, Patricia, et al. *Defending Diversity: Affirmative Action at the University of Michigan*. Ann Arbor: University of Michigan Press, 2004.

Gutman, Arthur. *EEP Law and Personnel Practices*. Thousand Oaks, CA: Sage Publications, 2000.

Holzer, Harry J. "Affirmative Action After Grutter: Still Worth Preserving?" *George Mason University Civil Rights Law Journal*, Spring 2004, pp. 217–228.

Kang, Jerry. "Trojan Horses of Race." *Harvard Law Review*, March 2005, pp. 1489–1593.

Laird, Bob. *The Case for Affirmative Action in University Admissions*. Berkeley, CA: Bay Tree Publishing, 2005.

Ong, Paul, ed. *Impacts of Affirmative Action: Policies and Consequences in California*. Walnut Creek, CA: AltaMira Press, 1999.

Pincus, Fred L. *Reverse Discrimination: Dismantling the Myth*. Boulder, CO: Lynne Rienner, 2003.

Rosenfeld, Michel. *Affirmative Action and Justice: A Philosophical and Constitutional Inquiry*. New Haven: Yale University Press, 1991.

Ruethling, Gretchen. "National Briefing Midwest—Michigan: Minorities Protest Program." *New York Times*, September 30, 2004, p. A26.

Sander, Richard H. "A Systemic Analysis of Affirmative Action in American Law Schools," *Stanford Law Review*, November 2004, pp. 367–483.

Bibliography

Selmi, M. "The Life of Bakke: An Affirmative Action Retrospective." *Georgetown Law Journal*, April 1999, pp. 981–1022.

Stohr, Greg. *A Black and White Case: How Affirmative Action Survived Its Greatest Legal Challenge*. Princeton, NJ: Bloomberg Press, 2004.

Taylor, Bron Raymond. *Affirmative Action at Work: Law, Politics, and Ethics*. Pittsburgh, PA: University of Pittsburgh Press, 1991.

Winter, Greg. "National Briefing Midwest—Michigan: Black Enrollment Drops." *New York Times*, October 15, 2004, p. A23.

Wise, Tim J. *Affirmative Action: Racial Preference in Black and White*. New York: Routledge, 2005.

Young, John W. "The Impact of an SES-Based Model on a College's Undergraduate Admissions Outcomes." *Research in Higher Education*, November 2004, p. 777.

Zuriff, G. E. "Is Affirmative Action Fair?" *American Psychologist*, February-March, 2004, pp. 124–126.

Index

Page numbers in **boldface** are illustrations.

Adarand Constructors, Inc. v. Peña, 34, 52, 70, 87–88, 99
affirmative action, 7, 11–13
  backlash, 35
  ballot initiatives, 100–104, **101**, 102
  con debate, 11, 14, **15**, 59–77
  court cases, 7–9, 76, 77
  defining, 9–11
  historic beginnings, 26–31
  overturning, 31, 34
  percentage plans, 35, 54, 103–104
  policy issues, 7, 16, 59, 76, 88–93, 96, 108–109
  pro debate, 11, 14, 37–58
  special programs, 10
  as temporary measure, 75, 77, 93, 104, 113
  underlying problems and, 71–73
  voluntary plans, 80
African American, 13–14, 16–17, **22**, 42, 45–51, 73, 106–107, 109
  affirmative action and, 28, **29**, 32–33, 46, 56, 68–72, 77, 80–81, 93, 100
  historic discrimination, 18–21, **19**, 24, 37, 62, 65, 67, 82, 84
Age Discrimination in

Index

Employment Act of 1967, 13
Alabama Department of Public Safety, 82
American College Test (ACT), 89
Americans with Disabilities Act, 13
Anderson, Elizabeth, 56
antidiscrimination laws, 12–13
Asian/Pacific Americans, 17, 28, 45, 65, **66**, 67, 71, 74, 100
Association of American Medical Colleges (AAMC), 30, 41

Bakke, Allan, 78, 79
Bickel, Alexander, 84
bigotry, 19, 42, 45–46, 56, 59, 62, 109
Birgeneau, Robert, 100
Black Enterprise magazine, 40–41
Blackmun, Harry, 79, 82, 84, 85
Bok, Derek, 56
Bowen, William, 14, 47, 53–56
Bradley, Joseph, 23
Brennan, William, 79, 82, 84, 85
broadcasting industry, 85–87
Brown v. Board of Education, 24–25
Burger, Warren, 78, 81

Bush, George, 31
Bush, Jeb, 35
business, 12–13, 78, 85–88, 99
 diversity in, 40–41, 50–52, 75, 77, 98–99
 government contracts, 10, 11, 100
 minority, 28, 31, 34, 81–83, 99

California Board of Regents, 35
California Proposition 209, 35, 100, **101**, **102**
Canisius College, 73
carpetbagger, 21, 23
Carter, Jimmy, 28, 47
Center for Individual Rights (CIR), 35, 74, 76, 109
certiorari, petition for, 94, 95
chauvinism, 43, 59, 62
City of Richmond v. Croson, 31, 83–85
civil rights, 11, 24–25, 33, 46, 62
 laws, 12–13, 21, 23, 25–27, 60, 77, 81, 89, 109, **112**
Civil Rights Act of 1866, 21
Civil Rights Act of 1875, 23
Civil Rights Act of 1964, 12, 25–27
Civil Rights Act of 1991, 12–13, 85
Civil Rights Cases of 1883, 23, 25
civil rights movement, 24–26, 42
Cleveland Bar Association, 110
Cleveland Minority Clerkship Program, 110–111
Clinton, Bill, 34, 41
color-blindness, 57, 60, 81, 92

137

Affirmative Action

Compromise of 1877, 23
Connerly, Ward, 14, 35, 69–70, 103–104, **105**
Cox, Michael, 7
crime rates, 48, 106
critical mass of minorities, 91, 98

Defunis v. Odegaard, 95
demographics, 15–17, 47–51, 54, 107
Department of Housing and Urban Development, 74
Department of Transportation, 87
depositive motion, 94
disadvantaged, 52–53, 61, 73, 78–79, 84, 87–88, 99, 108
discrimination, 11–14, 50, 58, 99
  affirmative action as, 60–62, 63
  benign, 70, 79, 83, 85–88
  legal recourse, 76, 77, 85
  ongoing, 42–45, 84, 109
  remediating, 75, 79–81, 82–85, 87
  through American history, 18–20, **19**, 24–26, 30, 34, 46–47, 52, 62, 65, 67
diversity, 38–42, 47, 54–55, 58, 85–86, 91–92, 98–99, 103–104
Diversity Scholarship, 8
Donelon, Clement, 16

Douglas, William, 63, 75
due process, 12, 21, 95

education, 13, 20, 26, 48, 57
  admission factors, 53–58, 64, 72–73, 78–80, 88–93, 96–98, 100, 103–104
  affirmative action programs and, 9–12, 30–32, 40, 59, 100
  college performance, 68–69, 71–73, 75, 109
  credentials, 55, 58, 69, 75, 76
  fostering diversity, 39–40, 47, 54–55, 58, 79–80, 91–92, 98, 103–104
  need policies, 49
Educational Amendments of 1972, 13
  Title IX, 26
Elder, Larry, 14, 68, 69
Equal Employment Opportunity Commission, 16, 42, 77
equal opportunity, 11, 13, 17, 25, 31–33, 59, 62, 74, 103, 113
  in business, 40, 49–50, 75, 99
Equal Pay Act of 1963, 12, 26
equal protection of law, 12, 21, 60, 62, 74–75, 86–88, 93
ethnicity, 9–10, 13–14, 19, 27–28, 30, 45, 47, 49, 52, 54, 60, 62–64, 67, 74, 79, 85–86, 89,

Index

91, 93, 96, 98, 100, 106
achievement and, 71, 73, 108
Executive Order 10925, 26
Executive Order 11246, 27, 31
Executive Order 11375, 27, 31

family structure, 47, 107–108
Federal Communications Commission (FCC), 85, 86
federal funding, 12–13, 25–26, 106–107
Ferguson, Ronald, 109
Fletcher, Arthur, 27
Frederickson, H. George, 52, 53
Fullilove v. *Klutznick*, 81

gender, 9–13, 26–27, 50, 52, 60, 62, 64–65, 83, 97, 106
gender-neutral program, 74
Ginsburg, Ruth Bader, 14, 46, 58, 88, 91, 113
glass ceiling, 43, 77
Gonzales Construction Company, 87
good old boy network, 51
government contracts, 10–12, 27–28, 29, 31, 34, 49, 59–60, 64–65
 Supreme Court and, 78, 83–85, 99
Gratz, Jennifer, 76, 89, 91
Gratz v. *Bollinger*, 89
Greenwald, Anthony, 45
Grutter, Barbara, 76, **90**
Grutter v. *Bollinger*, 88, 113

Guinier, Lani, 56

Hamacher, Patrick, 76, 89, 91
Hammonds, Evelynn, 43
Harlan, John, 60
Hayes, Rutherford B., 23
Hispanics, 15, 17, 28, 45, 47–51, 67, 71, 73–74, 77, 100
Homestead Act of 1862, 50
Hopwood v. *Texas*, 35

immigration, 19, 65
individuals vs. groups, 62–64, 69–70, 86–87, 92
Initiative 200, 35
integration, 53, 56

Jim Crow era, 24, 42, 50
job opportunities, 8, 10–13, 20, 26–27, 30, 32, 45–46, 48–51, 57, 59–60, 72, 74, 106
 women and, 20, 25–26, 28, 42–43, 48–49, 75, 77
Johnson, Andrew, 21
Johnson, Lyndon B., 27, 32–33
Johnson v. *Transportation Agency*, 82–83
Jordan, Eddie, 16

Kaiser Aluminum, 80
Kaiser-USWA plan, 80, 81
Kennedy, Anthony, 61, 87
Kennedy, John F., 26, 27
King, Martin Luther Jr., 46

Affirmative Action

Know-Nothing Party, 19–20
Ku Klux Klan, **112**
Kurzweil, Martin, 39, 54, 55, 106

Labor Department Order No. 4, 27
Laird, Bob, 14, 45, 49, 53
Lincoln, Abraham, 20
Long, Donnie, 111
lynchings, 24, 42, 65

manifest imbalances, correcting, 80–83
Marshall, Thurgood, 47, 79, 82, 84, 85
median family income, 48–49
merit system, 64–65
Metro Broadcasting, Inc. v. *FCC*, 85–87
Michigan Civil Rights Institute, 103
minority business enterprises (MBE), 28, 31, 34, 81–83, 99
model minority, **66**
mommy track, 42
Murphy, J. Harold, 8

National Center for Policy Analysis, 100
Native American, 19, 21, 28, 71
Naturalization Act of 1790, 50
networking, 51, 52

net worth statistics, 48, 51
Nixon, Richard, 27
No Child Left Behind Act, 106

O'Connor, Sandra Day, 51, 61, 83, 84, 86, 88, 92, 104
One Florida, 35
Oregon State University, 40

Pell, Terrence, 69, 71–72, 76, 109
personal responsibility, 108, 109
Philadelphia Order, 27
Plessy v. *Ferguson*, 24, 60
poll tax, 24, 25
poverty rates, 47–48, 73, 106, 108
Powell, Lewis, 79, 80, 82, 92
preferential treatment, 10–11, 13, 28, 50, 61–62, 65–66, 85, 88, 99
 college admission, 39, 47, 53–56, 58, 80, 89, 93, 97, 100, 104
 women and, 75, 77, 97
prejudice, 12–13, 19, 27, 45, 57, 65, 70, 79, 82, 109, 111, **112**
presidential election of 1876, 23
President's Committee on Equal Employment

Index

Opportunity, 26
privilege, white male, 49–52, 61
professions, diversity in, 41, 47–48, 50–51, 75, 110–111
public benefits, distributing, 52–53, 81, 86
public good, 53, 56
public interest law firms, 76
public scrutiny, 96
Public Works Employment Act, 28, 81

quotas, 13, 26, **29**, 30, 78, 80–84, 96, 97

race, 8–10, 16, 30–31, 35, 39, 52, 54, 58, 60, 62, 92–93, 106
  paternalism, 70–71, 88
  perceptions, 13–14, 15, 40
  preference, 65, 79, 88–89, 93, 100, 104
race discrimination, 16, 27, 47, 50, 61, 67, 70, 82, 85, 93
race-neutral program, 74, 84, 103
racial classification, 74–75, 79, 84–88
racism, 45–46, 60–62, 69–70, 72, 113

Reagan, Ronald, 31
Reconstruction Era, 21, **22**, 23, 24
recruitment visits, 10, 103
redlining, 50
Regents of the University of California v. Bakke, 78, 92, 94, 96
Rehabilitation Act of 1973, 13
Rehnquist, William, 78, 93, 96
reverse discrimination, 7, 11
Rockwell, Paul, **102**

Sander, Richard, 68
Santa Clara County, 82
Scalia, Antonin, 61, 62, 84, 88
Scholastic Aptitude Test (SAT), 49, 56, 57, 89
segregation, 8, 24, 47, 54, 65, 77, 83
separate but equal, 24, 25, 60
set aside programs, 28, **29**, 34, 53, 78–79, 82–83
sexual harassment, 42, 45, 75
Shaw, Theodore, 41
Shuller, G. Phillip III, 16
single-parenthood, 107–108
slavery, 18–21, 23, 50, 61, 65
Small Business Act, 28, 34
Small Business Administration (SBA), 99
socioeconomic status, 47–51,

141

Affirmative Action

54–55, 58, 60, 73, 106–108
Souter, David, 52, 91
standardized tests, 49, 56–57, 63–65, 69, 107
status quo, 82, 109
Steelworkers v. Weber, 80
stereotypes, 43, 45, 49, 56, 63, 92, 109
Stevens, John Paul, 61, 78, 82, 88
Stewart, Potter, 78–79
stigma, 61, 67
strict scrutiny, 83–85, 86, 87, 88
Sturm, Susan, 56
suburbia, 50–51
Summers, Lawrence, 43, **44**

Talented Twenty program, 35, 104
Taxman, Sharon, 7
Thomas, Clarence, 14, **15**, 70, 88, 91, 93
Tilden, Samuel, 23
Tobin, Eugene, 54
Tompkins, Jessie, 8, 9
tracking programs, 30–31, 34, 42–43, 79
trickle down effect, 72
Truman, Harry, 24

U.S. Constitution, 12, 60, 62, 79, 81, 83–84, 87, 89
Article I, 25
First Amendment, 80
Twelfth Amendment, 20, 23
Fourteenth Amendment, 12, 20–21, 25, 60, 79, 82, 86, 88
Fifteenth Amendment, 21
Nineteenth Amendment, 20
Twenty-Fourth Amendment, 25
U.S. military, 24
U.S. Supreme Court, 13, 31, 34, **38**, 78–96
road to, 94–95
United States v. Paradise, 82
United Steelworkers of America, 80
University of California
at Berkeley, 100, **101**
at Davis, 31, 78–80, 107
University of Michigan, 35–36, 39–40, 76, 88–93, **90**, 96, 98
College of Literature, Arts and Sciences (LAS), 36, 89, 91

Index

Law School, 36, 88, **90**, 91–92, 96
Urban Institute 2004 study, 71–72

voting rights, **19**, 20–25, **22**, 32
Voting Rights Act of 1965, 25

Wagmiller, Robert, 51
White, Byron, 79
white/European ethnic group, 15, 46–50, 56, 62, 65, 71–73, 76–78, 80–81, 89, 100, 106–107, 109
white guilt, 37
Williams, Debra, 7
Wilson, William Julius, 107
Wise, Tim, 50, 51
women, 9, 12, 25–28, 30–31, 37, 42–48, **44**, 50–51, 56, 65, 67, 72, 82, 109
 achievement, 75, 77
women business enterprises (WBEs), 28
women's suffrage, **19**, 20, 26 suffrage, **19**, 20, 26

About the Author

Kathiann M. Kowalski has written seventeen books and approximately 400 articles and stories for young people. She has written *Global Warming* and *Taxes*, books in the Marshall Cavendish Benchmark Open for Debate series. Kowalski received her bachelor's degree in political science from Hofstra University and her law degree from Harvard Law School, where she was an editor of the *Harvard Law Review*. Kowalski has spent fifteen years practicing law and over ten years writing books. Her books have won awards from the Society of School Librarians International, the American Society for the Prevention of Cruelty to Animals, the Pennsylvania School Librarians Association (PSLA), the National Science Teachers Association, and the Children's Book Council.